All the best to You
both !

Al Hedix

MANAGEMENT FOR THE CHRISTIAN WORKER

Written by
OLAN HENDRIX

Illustrated by
WAYNE STAYSKAL

Quill Publications
117 West Lake Street, Libertyville, Illinois

**This book is dedicated
to
Elizabeth**

TABLE OF CONTENTS

Published by Quill Publications
117 West Lake, Libertyville, Ill. 60048 U.S.A.

Library of Congress Catalog Card No. 76-3510
ISBN 0-916608-01-8

WHAT IS QUILL PUBLICATIONS?

A few years back a need was seen to help authors of merit find a means to bring their ideas to the attention of the public. Some of these authors had developed reputations based on previous writings, lectures and professional expertise, but many were new, young writers never having published, but with fresh ideas. Quill Publications was established to help those writers of merit reach the people that could best benefit from their knowledge and experience. Consequently, we have had enthusiastic support from educators, media people, artists and most important, you the reader. We are concerned that our publications are of high quality and readily available. At present we are attempting to find new works by good writers. These works may be fiction or non-fiction, textbooks or self help materials. It is from you the readers of our present publications that we are hoping to get these future books. We are interested in discussing with writers their ideas as they touch man's relationship to God, to himself, to his fellow man, and to his environment. If you feel you have something to contribute, we would like to hear from you.

FOREWARD

Many churches have been seriously damaged and the work of a number of Christian institutions has been handicapped by well-meaning and spiritually minded men who have never learned the principles of effective management.

When many of us were students in theological seminaries who are now in the pastoral ministry or in some other type of Christian service in which we have management responsibilities, there were no courses offered in church management. Ministers were expected to be able to manage others by virtue of their high calling. Perhaps partly as a consequence of this viewpoint, there are some in the pastoral ministry today who sincerely believe that dependence upon the Holy Spirit is all that is necessary in working with other people. They consider any effort to learn and perfect skills in the management of others as unspiritual.

Most ministers and Christian workers today recognize that to be effective in the proclamation of the gospel, men need extensive training in communication skills. This we call homiletics in the theological seminary. Similarly, to be able to handle adequately the responsibilities of the pastorate or the direction of a mission agency or the administration of a Christian educational institution, one must learn the skills of good management. Fortunately, many evangelical theological seminaries today are recognizing the importance of including courses in management in their regular curriculum.

A theological seminary education is not designed to teach a man all he needs to know about the Bible in order to be an effective minister. It is designed to give him the tools for life-long study and ministry of the Word of God. Similarly, no course in management nor book on the subject can provide a Christian worker all the information he needs to be successful in managing the work of other people. However, the principles of management set forth in this book provide the tools for spiritual men to use for the glory of God and for the effective conduct of the work of the church just as they use the principles of homiletics in preparing effective sermons.

The author of this volume, the Reverend Olan Hendrix, is highly qualified to write on this subject. He has had wide experience in the pastorate and extensive participation in the work of missions as an executive in several missionary organizations. He has served as a management consultant for a number of Christian organizations and is a member of the board of directors of the West Indies Mission and Wycliffe Associates. He has conducted management seminars in many parts of the world. National church leaders as well as missionaries have expressed profound appreciation for the assistance they have received from his lectures.

Although he has studied extensively the large amount of management literature available today, Mr. Hendrix subjects all the principles of management advocated by others to the authority of the Word of God. His approach to the problems of management is thoroughly Biblical. I heartily commend this book to pastors and Christian workers.

Robert G. Rayburn,
President and Professor of Practical Theology
Covenant Theological Seminary
12330 Conway Road
St. Louis, Missouri 63141

November 24, 1975

INTRODUCTION

When I began my ministry more than a quarter of a century ago, management was the furthest thing from my mind. All I ever wanted to do was preach and teach. And I wanted to do it in China. That was in the mid-40's before China closed its doors to foreigners. My career took strange but exciting and rewarding turns. A total of ten years in the pastorate, ten years on the home staff of a foreign mission society, and almost six years as director of a large home mission.

Early in my career I found that the ministry involved more than preaching. This book has to do with one, just one, of the often neglected ingredients for a fruitful ministry.

It is easy to see that many of our problems are spiritual. In recent years we have even begun to admit that some are cultural. But, how slowly we have come to see that clearly a large segment of our problems are management in nature. This book attempts to offer some help in the latter area only.

This book has a curious history. I delivered some management lectures in Kenya. Then an excited missionary from Zaire typed word-for-word those five days of talks. Later a man from the North of Ireland edited the copy, and a religious publishing company in India printed the first edition in 1970. Now this very much revised, updated and enlarged edition is made available here in the states.

I am sure that my management thinking has evolved through the years, what with lecturing to well over 8,000 church leaders in 28 countries over a period of almost 15 years. However, this little volume will introduce the subject and will serve as a useful tool to acquaint fellow workers in your church, mission or other type of Christian organization with management work.

One more thing! Please make no assumptions regarding the author's personal perfection in the practice of management. I have studied the subject avidly because I needed to. I still need to! All you need to do is ask the people with whom I have worked these years. But I refuse to allow my own management imperfections to deter me from sharing all I can with you. The same principle applies in preaching. Every great preacher preaches beyond his experience. Just as an over-developed sense of perfectionism is always one of the greatest enemies to management work, so it could easily silence me on the subject. I refuse!

We face a broken world in unspeakable need. And you and I need all the help we can get. Management skills and tools *can* help.

Olan Hendrix

Marion Station, PA
1975

CHAPTER 1

UNDERSTAND
THE PROBLEM

The Case for Management
in the Christian Organization

THE CASE FOR MANAGEMENT
IN THE CHRISTIAN ORGANIZATION

"It appears to me that management in Christian circles is basically the stewardship of the talents of the persons entrusted to our care."

We are faced with a subject which for some of us is going to be new. Let me suggest the kinds of questions that are going to come to your mind. You are going to wonder first, "Is the subject of management spiritual or is it a carnal deviation from trusting the Holy Spirit?" You are going to wonder, "Is it Biblical? Is there a Biblical basis of management principles? How can this apply to Christian work?" People often say, "Management is all very good, but how can you apply it when you don't sign the man's paycheck every week, and don't have the right to fire him?" There are definite answers to these and other questions. However, do not let doubts or uncertainties prevent you from receiving the instruction which can answer these questions. We can easily close our minds so that there is no possibility of learning. Though the subject of Christian management is relatively new and something of an innovation, clear instruction and help is available for spiritual men.

First, a definition — what do we mean by management? The word "management" may sound too authoritative, or too worldly, for you. Then choose you own word. It does not matter what words we use so long as we understand what is meant by this word. We may talk about the boss, the director, the superintendent, the supervisor, the leader, or the manager. This is beside the point. The person in charge of a group of human beings for the accomplishment of a mutually agreed purpose is the manager. In this book I will use the words management and leadership quite interchangeably, although management is a much more encompassing word of which leadership is just a part.

The Stewardship of Talents

Let me suggest several definitions. It appears to me that management in Christian circles is basically the stewardship of the talents of the persons entrusted to our care. Regardless of where you are, you work with people. If you are in a position of leadership at all, you may not have much to say about who these people are and you certainly have very little to say about what their capacities or gifts are. However, you bear a solemn responsibility to exercise the stewardship of the talents of those people God has entrusted to your care. Basically, it is not for you to choose — and we often would choose men with different capacities if we had the option — but we do have the responsibility of exercising careful stewardship of the talents of these people.

In missions and church activities I have observed serious abuse at this point. We often disregard a man's God-given capacity and gifts, sometimes to the satisfaction of our own prejudices, and attempt to force these people into moulds or activities for which God the Holy Spirit has not equipped them. Our job as leaders is to exercise Spirit-directed stewardship over these talents. It is for the Christian manager to increase to the utmost the performance of those that God has brought into his ranks, taking into account his personal gifts and capacities.

Getting Things Done Through Other People

Lawrence A. Appley says, "Management is getting things done through other people." How is this important for us in Christian work? I am tremendously impressed with this. If ever anything is to be done in this broken world of ours, it is going to be done as we, who are called and sent of God, develop the awareness of the necessity for getting things done through other people. We *must* involve other people. I discovered soon after God saved me that I was never going to be able to accomplish the burden of my own life all by myself. I was going to have to involve myself with other people and I couldn't let myself and those entrusted to me do whatever struck my fancy, but *prescribed things* had to be done. It is so much easier, in fact, it is the coward's way out, to conclude that we are going to do what we can do by ourselves and we are not going to worry about what anybody else does.

I had a friend, a pastor of a little church in Maine, U.S.A. He had been there for years preaching to a handful of people. I asked him one day, "What in the world are you doing?" He was doing every menial task in the church, many of which could have been turned over to high school students and to others in the church. His answer appeared pious and commendable. Actually, it was disheartening. He said, "I do everything myself. I run off my own bulletins. I wash the windows in the church. I put out the hymn books. I do everything myself. This way I know it is done properly." We must develop the mentality, the attitude, that makes us want to involve other people so that much more can be accomplished and sooner. Jesus Christ did this. Our ministry is not only directed to people but it also involves accomplishing our purpose through people. It is not only *my* ministry to this broken world, but it is my reproducing myself in people with whom I am closely associated so that they minister to this broken world too. So, by way of definition I would insist that *management for the Christian worker is getting things done through other people.*

Basically, management is a set of skills that an ordinary person can acquire and develop. But management may also be thought of as a kind of work which you learn to perform. The important word as we study management is WORK — a kind of work which we perform. The whole emphasis in the next few pages is going to be upon this idea.

You see someone effectively managing or leading a group of people and you are apt to think, "That looks easy. Let me get at it. I can do that." So we jump in and try. Recently friends were visiting us in Philadelphia. I took their teen-age boys water-skiing along with my own boys. One boy, about 15 years old, said, "I'd like to ski too." I asked, "Do you know how, Bobby?" "Oh, yes, yes." So I agreed. He got out and I noticed that when I pulled the rope up taut, his skis were very uncertain, but I thought, "Well, he's a little shaky." Finally he got them straightened out and when I raced the engine, skis and legs and arms went all over the place! I pulled back around, harnessed him up and tried again — and again legs and arms and skis went in all directions. After about the fourth time I pulled back around by him and said, "Bobby, do you know how to ski?" "Yes, I know how to ski." I thought better of the question and said, "Bobby, have you ever ski'd?" And he replied, "No, but it looks easy." It is that way with leadership. You stand a few feet back and watch a fellow effectively leading a group and you think, "Oh, that's easy." You just smile, say a few words, write letters and lead meetings. You give orders and recieve reports and it is great — until you try it, and then it is not so easy! It requires skills that very few of us possess naturally.

Now, occasionally a man comes along who can "manage by the seat of his pants!" Let me explain that. Back in World War I, I am told, the pilots in the era preceding the fantastic navigational aids that we enjoy today used to tell whether they were flying right side up in the clouds or wrong side up by where the pressure was. If the pressure was on the seat of their pants, they were right side up! If the pressure was on their seat belts, they were wrong side up! Some of us in Christian work manage by the seats of our pants, that is, if it feels right, if it feels comfortable, then it's okay. Or, if intuitively or instinctively you think that is the thing to do or that is not the thing to do, we act accordingly. The problem here is that few people are equipped by conditioning, training, judgment or personality to manage this way. This is why we need to learn specific leadership skills. You must identify and then acquire these skills. I will try to show you how to go about acquiring them. We are looking at Christian management as work to be performed, as skills to be acquired.

On one occasion my six-year-old boy was trying to learn to ride a bicycle. Oh, what mistakes! You got him going, and he'd bang into the side of the house or into a tree or something else! One day he said, "Daddy, it looks so easy but it's hard." "It does look easy, John, but there are things you have to do. You have to keep going. You have to keep the wheels going in the right direction. You need to steer and feel the balance. When you feel the bike going one way you have to pull back the other way." He said, "Yes, but it looks so easy." There are a lot of things that look easy but they require learning certain skills. There are times when you develop these skills to where they become second nature. They become instinctive. You are not conscious that you are practicing these skills — like riding a bicycle. After a while, though, it becomes second nature. You just do it — but first you learn the skill and then you abide by the rules.

Tools for Spiritual Men

Management is a skill, but it is also a set of tools for spiritual men. Management tools can be used by people who are not spiritual for ulterior and worldly purposes. But, by the same token, spiritual men can take these tools and use them for the glory of God and for the furtherance of the work of Jesus Christ. The point is not whether these tools are spiritual or not — *the whole point is whether WE are spiritual or not.* Let us not argue with the skills or the tools but with the condition of our own hearts. The issue is, "Am I a spiritual man?" If so, these tools can be worthwhile and powerful implements in our hands.

Now if you want to be carnal in your service for Jesus Christ, you do not have to use management skills in order to be so. In a slovenly way, in a haphazard way, you can be carnal. The using of these skills does not mean that you are carnal, nor does the absence of them mean that you are spiritual. Be careful about that assumption.

Management as a Supplement

Here is a quotation that I want to sink so deeply into your consciousness that you will never, never forget it. An Ohio pastor made this observation — *"There are some things God will bless as a supplement that He will curse as a substitute."* I am not talking about management skills as a substitution for anything.

Often people will wonder:

"Isn't this a substitute for the fullness of the Holy Spirit?" No!

"Isn't this a bypassing of the responsibilities for the exposition of the Word?" No!

"Isn't this a shortcut to try to circumvent the necessity for believers being drawn together in spiritual unity?" No!

Management is not a substitute for anything. It is a *supplement*. It is a set of tools for spiritual men.

It is so important that we understand one another, that we get started off right and on the right foundation. The issue is not the spirituality of management. The issue is the spirituality of the man. We spend our lives arguing about the spirituality of things. Things are not spiritual; men are.

Management in the Bible

Is the subject of management scriptural? — Is it Biblical? Can we honestly study this subject giving the Word of God the pre-eminence in guiding our thinking? I think we can. I believe that every basic, honorable principle in management has its root and foundation in the Word of God.

The Life of Joseph

Take, for example, the life of Joseph. Is there in all of history a more magnificent example of leadership and good management than Joseph? Preparing for that monumental harvest, then the horrible years of famine, delegating, planning the whole operation, distributing the materials, the foodstuffs, satisfying the complaints and handling the grievances — all are there. The people he had to work with were no better than the people you and I work with. As a matter of fact, he might have had worse people than some of us have. A magnificent example of organization in Scripture! And did God just drop it down into his brain so that he did it instinctively without ever thinking? I do not think so. God seldom works that way with men. Generally, He will guide us to the subjects we need to study and learn.

Nehemiah and His Exploits

Or take Nehemiah and his exploits. If you read the book of Nehemiah carefully, and seek to find the management principles in it, you will discover that it contains every major management principle we know about today.

If I were to give a biblical exposition on the subject of management I would unhesitatingly turn to the book of Nehemiah. It is all there in lucid and succinct form.

Jesus and His Relationships

Is there organization in Scripture? I think so. Dr. Robert Coleman in his book, *The Master Plan of Evangelism*, studies the life of the Lord Jesus in His relationship with the apostles, and shows His selection of them, then His association with them, impartation, demonstration, delegation, supervision and reproduction. There were intense organizational activities in the life of the Lord Jesus and in His relations with His disciples. Of course, the classic source of information regarding the Lord and His twelve is the volume by A.B. Bruce, *The Training of the Twelve.*

I attended a management seminar taught by Louis A. Allen, a noted management researcher. When he came to the subject of delegation he said, "I've got one example of delegation for you—Moses." This is a classic example of delegation in the Word of God. Delegation did not solve all the problems for Moses, but it solved some of the major ones. It created some others, but any time you solve one problem you create other problems. In fact, the last question you always ask yourself when you implement a decision to solve a problem is, "What is going to go wrong when I implement this decision?" Any time you solve one problem, you are probably going to create some others.

Confident Christian Leadership

I want to point out something about management in the Church of the Lord Jesus Christ. *It would mean a lot to the security of our people if they looked to us and found us confident.* "This is the work God has given me to do." It is Biblical, is it not? God gives these various capacities to men and then He gives men to the Church for specific purposes (Eph. 4:11-12). Romans 12:8 says, "Or he that exhorteth, let him wait on exhortation; he that giveth, let him do it with simplicity; he that ruleth, with diligence." (A.V.) The Cambridge Bible says "ruleth" means to "preside whether in church or in any point of the work." It goes on to say that "with diligence" means "in haste, with earnestness, with laborious and minute attention to duty." It is always interesting to me that we are so apologetic in our attitude toward our positions of responsibility. Why is this? I think there are some reasons for it psychologically. We need to put our shoulders back and hold our heads high and say, "I am the pastor, I am the leader, I am whatever I am by the appointment of a sovereign God." We often underestimate ourselves and cause others to value us below God's estimation of us. I am not suggesting that we grasp after position. We are not to count the position as something to be grasped after. No, we are to have the mind of Christ. But we are not talking about status. We are talking about work, about a divine assignment of work and a performance of skills. What happens if we belittle our ability and position? This is one of the reasons we are in trouble in evangelicalism, because we have underestimated our leadership ability.

Why Has Management Been Neglected?

The next thing to consider is, "Why is this subject neglected?" The first reason is *ignorance.* We simply do not know how to manage. It never occurred to most of us to study leadership as a set of skills that might be acquired like you study apologetics or hermeneutics. My orientation was preaching. That is all I ever wanted to do. But, I got out of bed one morning and found myself a manager! I was not alone — other people in our mission were in the same boat. What do you do? You "fly by the seat of your pants!" You do what you feel is right or what you think is right or what you hope is right. Of course you pray and ask for guidance, but basically you are ignorant of what to do.

One day one of my board members came along and said, "Olan, you are in trouble." I knew that. My only consolation was that I was not alone. Our mission had outgrown a very satisfactory form of management. Normally an organization comes into being with a certain form of government. However, it will outgrow the demand for that style of leadership and demand a new style of leadership as it goes through various structures and stages. This is why most organizations emerge, flourish, and then founder! They cannot make the transition into a new era. We were in real trouble — demoralization had set in. Our best men were threatening to leave. Our form of government seemed to be working against us.

So this board member came along and said, "If I pay your way to a management seminar, will you go?" Well, at that point I would have jumped off a bridge if I thought it would have helped. We were in trouble. So I attended a seminar, and as I sat there and listened to the leader talk about the application of management principles to co-operative human efforts I said, "That will work! That is our problem! There is where we have missed it!" The ignorance began to be dispelled. It was not easy. I had a lot of ingrained prejudices and I had to overcome them, and I am still having to overcome them.

Another reason why we neglect this subject is that our traditional concept of leadership in the church is *the Strong Natural Leader.* Now when God saved me and called me to preach, all I wanted to do was preach. I wanted to learn how to preach, and especially how to be a missionary. Later, when I knew I could not go to China, I wanted to learn how to be a pastor. I thought to myself, "I am going to learn how to preach and how to get things done." So I went away to college. And, lo and behold, at this college there was a Strong Natural Leader in charge. The college was also in close proximity to a large church. I decided I was going to watch how he became so great.

He would get up in church and let his congregation have it straight from the shoulder! I decided I could do the same thing. So when I got the opportunity to preach out in a small country church, I would get up and let them have it straight from the shoulder, and they would toss me out by my ear! I would then pull myself together and go back the next Sunday to observe him and say, "I'll watch some more. I missed something." Again, he would let them have it straight from the shoulder. I have seen that man get up and call on four or five deacons to pray when he knew they were not there, just to embarrass them in front of 2,000 people. Well, what I did not know was that this man was a Strong Natural Leader, and he can't be copied. But how can we know?

A student came along one time when I was in college, looked at my library such as it was, and said, "Look, all you have is Greek, Hebrew, apologetics and philosophy. Where are your biographies?" I replied, "Why do I need them? I am going to preach." He said, "You need to read biographies." So I went out and bought some biographies and autobiographies. You know, most biographies are written about Strong Natural Leaders. They did not help me. Reading those biographies hindered me. I found myself spending some nights in prayer, asking God to make me one of them. I did not know the term

Strong Natural Leader then but I had Wesley, Taylor, Studd, Whitefield, Edwards, Spurgeon and others in mind. I wanted to be like them.

That is bondage. You have to accept yourself as you are. It was like getting out of jail when I awakened one day to discover that God wants me just as I am. I am not talking in a moral sense but in the sense of personality and capacity. God has made me as I am. God has equipped me as I am equipped. He has divided these gifts to every man according to His wisdom. Well, this was wonderful! But how slow we have been to recognize this.

The strong natural leader is often successful — highly successful — *but usually only over a short period of time.* Unless he dies or is displaced, he often becomes his organization's worst enemy. I was glad to discover that I was not a strong natural leader.

There is an alternative, and *the alternative is the professional leader,* the *scientific leader* or the *developed leader.* I mean, the man who does not have the dominating personality to draw people to himself automatically, to cause them to do what he wants them to do. But instead he is the person who is an ordinary human being like you or me who develops leadership skills and engages in this management work.

Now, I am not concerned with the Strong Natural Leader. He seldom attends a leadership conference or reads a management book like this. He feels he does not need to. Ordinary persons like you and me who are in positions of leadership can develop extensive leadership skills. That is the point that we are dealing with in the coming chapter: *how to develop these skills.* We want to discover how to implement these skills in the situations in which we find ourselves.

CHAPTER 2
IDENTIFY RESPONSIBILITIES
The Functions and Activities
of Management

THE FUNCTIONS AND ACTIVITIES OF MANAGEMENT

"In management, and especially in Christian management, you never come to the place where you can say, "I am finished." You are not building a table or a chair; you are working with lives, with human beings, with minds, with emotions, with hearts, with frail bodies subject to all the pressures of an ever changing world."

Every activity that is involved in any managerial situation can be plugged in under one of the following *four main headings* or one of the *nineteen subpoints.*[1] This is true in a highly complex managerial situation, such as General Motors, or in a simple situation. Even two people working together to accomplish a mutually agreed objective must accomplish the same activities.

I. FUNCTION: MANAGEMENT PLANNING
ACTIVITIES: Estimating the Future
Establishing objectives
Developing policies
Programming
Establishing procedures
Scheduling
Budgeting

1. Allen, Louis A. *The Management Profession.* Mc-Graw-Hill, page 68

II. FUNCTION: MANAGEMENT ORGANIZING
   ACTIVITIES: Developing organization structure
                 Delegating
                 Establishing Inter-Personal Human
                   Relationships

III. FUNCTION: MANAGEMENT LEADING
    ACTIVITIES: Decision making
                  Communicating
                  Motivating
                  Selecting people
                  Developing people

IV. FUNCTION: MANAGEMENT CONTROLLING
    ACTIVITIES: Establishing performance standards
                  Performance measuring
                  Performance evaluating
                  Performance correcting

The outline is broken down into four parts. Louis Allen calls them functions: Planning, Organizing, Leading, and Controlling. My purpose is to discuss this list, defining the terms very briefly with the hope that we can look into these subjects individually and see how they relate to Christian work.

This grouping is not in any order. You do not plan before you organize or before you lead or before you develop. These are just put down this way because you have to put them down some way. You can even set up a management file just like this — planning, leading, organizing and controlling. It makes a good acrostic—PLOC. I have a file for each of these main points and each of the subpoints. Everytime I find something on the subject of management that I want to retain I file it in one of these places. I find that everything written on the subject of management can fit easily into one of these slots.

What do we mean by these terms? I will give some very brief definitions.

I. MANAGEMENT PLANNING

PLANNING is the work we do to predetermine a course of action. Or, planning is throwing a net over tomorrow to cause to come to pass the thing we want to come to pass. The alternative to planning is chance and just letting things happen as they will.

ESTIMATING THE FUTURE is the work we do to anticipate what tomorrow is going to be like. Many of us say we do not know this because things change so rapidly. This is all the more reason why we need to engage in the work of estimating. Because of the rapidity with which changes are taking place today, we need to appraise as accurately as possible what tomorrow is going to be like.

The principle resource for doing this difficult work is the study of trends that affect our organizations. Trends are not infallible but they are the best indicator we have.

ESTABLISHING OBJECTIVES is the work we do to determine goals or targets. Any Christian organization that has been in existence for more than twenty years usually has no goals, just activities.

The hardest work we have to do in being the heart of an organization is determining cooperatively meaningful objectives. I seldom meet a pastor who can answer me in a few words, "Pastor, what is the objective of your church? Why is your church in existence?" You would be surprised how much confusion there is in respect to goals and objectives in Christian work. This, more than anything else, contributes to our ineffectiveness. You can be filled with the Holy Spirit and not have definitive goals in your work.

DEVELOPING POLICIES is the work of formulating standing answers to recurring questions. Normally, in Christian work we confuse policies and objectives. A potential missionary candidate will often ask, "What are your mission policies?" What he usually means is, "What are your mission objectives?"

PROGRAMMING is the establishing of the priority and sequence of activities for the accomplishment of our goals or objectives. Objectives should always sit in judgement on activites.

PROCEDURES is the standardizing of the methods of work. We are easily lax in Christian work in this area. A young man is thrown into a work and told to do it, but he is not allowed to benefit from what has been previously learned by other people who have gone before into similar types of work. Everybody should benefit from what others have learned about a particular type of work. I have actually seen this sort of thing happen: A young missionary out of language study is assigned a town and told, "Start a church here." Start a church? What do I do now? Here is a town completely secularized and materialistic and preoccupied, with no need of God or the Gospel, and this young man is supposed to start a church. No one tells him, "Here is all we have learned from what we have been doing so far. We still do not know everything, but here is what little we do know. We want you to benefit from it so that you can get the job done most economically in time and effort."

SCHEDULING is the work of putting a time factor on your program and inserting the calendar into the program with dates, hours and minutes. Let us attempt to understand the mind of the Lord when He expects a certain thing done and then let us try to cooperate with the Holy Spirit.

BUDGETING concerns more than just money! A new convert was asked by the treasurer of our mission, "What are your impressions of missionaries?" He had several. This man, an advertising executive, said, "The missionaries that I have met put proper evaluation on money, but no evaluation on time." I agree. We are talking about budgeting men, time, and equipment, as well as money. Budgeting is the application of all of your resources.

II. MANAGEMENT ORGANIZING

ORGANIZING is the work of grouping people and work so the work can best be performed by human beings. Whenever you think of organizing, you probably think of something like charts, blocks, lines — these blocks representing people and titles: Director, Superintendent, Chairman, Supervisor, etc.

Organizing is tying together activities under one person for the accomplishment of a specific goal. Organizing is necessary to prevent fragmentation and the dissipation of activities and energies. Unless we organize, we have people doing what is noble and right and good and commendable, but not bringing into strict discipline all of the activities of their lives and resources to accomplish a purpose. Organizing does not have to be complicated. It does not make any difference how you do it, whether you have a chart or not. It means each human being knows what work he is definitively responsible for. There are three aspects to organizing:

First, DEVELOPING ORGANIZATIONAL STRUCTURE. In developing the structure, we group and relate the work and we relate people to one another. This is relating people one to another in their *performance* and in their *authority,* not just in responsibility.

Second, DELEGATION. There is more mis-understanding about delegation perhaps than any other single aspect of management. Delegating is the assigning of things: (1) Responsibility, or if you prefer, work. (2) Authority, that is, showing a person how much authority he has, what kind of decisions he can make, and how far he can go. He must not only know what he is to do, but how much money he can spend, how many decisions he can make, how many people he can direct or control, and how much time he can devote to it. (3) Accountability, establishing lines of reporting. The person who delegates not only says, "Will you do this piece of work?" and "Here is the authority you need in order to perform that job." He also says, "I will check back with you Friday afternoon at two o'clock to see how you are making out."

We frequently fail to establish lines of accountability and delegation because we are afraid of people. Management involves us "eyeball to eyeball" with people in direct personal encounter. It takes time. We like to think we are too busy preaching and teaching to perform management work.

If we will blend harmoniously these three ingredients in delegation, we can improve the performance of our organization tremendously. But remember, you must have all three aspects for success: responsibility, authority, and accountability.

Third, ESTABLISHING RELATIONSHIPS. Management organizing is *establishing and maintaining interpersonal relations.* Those little boxes that we draw and those words that we write on paper and the nice neat little job descriptions that we make — all that is wonderful, except when we forget one thing — they represent people! People who become ill, people who become offended, people who get tired, people who become depressed. If you do not like both people and people's problems, *get out of management.* If your attitude, when a problem emerges or when a person fails, is, "Will these people never learn?" — it is better that you leave management to somebody else. Your attitude should be like that of the Lord Jesus to His disciples.

A.B. Bruce brings this Jesus attitude out very clearly in his book, *The Training of the Twelve.* Christ taught the disciples that same thing over and over again. Finally they began to grasp a little bit of what He was trying to say. It must be done day after day. In management, and especially in Christian management, you never come to the place where you can say, "I am finished." You are not building a table or a chair; you are working with lives, with human beings, with minds, with emotions, with hearts, with frail bodies subject to all the pressures of an ever changing world.

III. MANAGEMENT LEADING

Of all four functions, management leading is the most work and the least mechanical. When it comes to leading, we are much more involved with interpersonal relationships. Management leading is the work we do to inspire and to impel people to take specific action. It involves five areas:

First, DECISION MAKING. That is, problem identification and problem solving. Decision making is the work we do to arrive at judgments and conclusions. Decision making is not simply intuition. There is a specific process in which we engage in order to arrive at logical judgments and conclusions. Decision making is not mystical either. In fact, a mystic can make some very bad judgments. The fact we have feelings at a gut level does not ensure that we are going to arrive at proper judgments and conclusions.

Second, COMMUNICATING. This is the work in which we engage to arrive at an understanding between ourselves and other people concerning mutual needs and goals. Beware of confusing understanding with agreement. We suffer infinitely more management ill from mis-understanding than from disagreement.

Third, MOTIVATING is one of the biggest subjects on the list. This is the work we do to cause people to want to do what needs to be done. Remember, significant motivating work is done one on one much more than in groups.

Fourth, SELECTING PEOPLE. This is the work in which we engage in order to appraise people's God-given capacities and the opportunities available to fit them. We try to find work for which individuals are best suited. How many misplaced Christian workers there are!

Fifth, DEVELOPING PEOPLE. This has to do with the work we do to upgrade the capacities for work and service which have been given by the Holy Spirit. Here is a man who has been equipped or gifted to do something special. To develop him we help enlarge those capacities and then build upon them. This is developing people.

IV. MANAGEMENT CONTROLLING

We define controlling as the work we do to insure that results conform to plan. Controlling presupposes both objectives and a specific structure. *Management controlling* has to do with the following four activities:

First, ESTABLISHING PERFORMANCE STANDARDS. Now, this means that we agree with the person or the persons working with us as to what quality work is going to be accomplished, before it is begun. There is a mutual agreement. Here is the job and here is the standard to which it is going to be performed. Many problems arise at this point. You give a man a job or ask him to do something. He assumes, "This is not very important. I can do it sloppily or half-heartedly. It does not really matter." We, however, attach a great deal of significance to it. We must adequately communicate in order that we agree about the standard for the job, otherwise there is going to be incompatibility and serious friction. We must establish performance standards. If a new assistant is assigned to you, let him know what you expect of him. What breaches of relationships occur because of failure to communicate expectations!

Second, PERFORMANCE MEASURING. This means that whether a fellow is counting money, passing out literature on the street, planting a church in a pioneer area, or whatever he is doing, somebody is measuring his work. Now, the point here is not to measure how many souls he has led to Christ; it is his performance in his work that is to be measured, and it may or may not be reflected in souls saved. We have built-in resistance when we attempt to do this.

Third, PERFORMANCE EVALUATING is the work we do to appraise the importance of this individual's work in relation to all of the other work which is being performed in the organization, and with respect to accomplishing the total goal. Get into this kind of thing seriously and you will find a lot of people doing jobs that do not need to be done.

Fourth, PERFORMANCE CORRECTING involves not only correcting mistakes that have been made, but also it involves coaching, providing the person with the "how." It is saying to him, "Here is how you do it," and then coming back to him to correct mistakes and to continually provide him with methods for accomplishing his work. You do not have to know how to do it yourself, but you have to know where to send him for the help he needs in order to learn how to do it. Performance correcting includes coaching. In other words, we do not just set standards, and measure and evaluate. We also coach: "Read that book." "Take that course." "Talk to that person." "Read this article."

According to L.A. Allen the above constitutes the totality of the management process in any and all situations. Your first love is likely to be preaching or teaching, but you have an inescapable responsibility to serve your people by doing management work for them. And if you do not incorporate this work in your life the entire organization will suffer.

THE BASIC ORGANIZATIONAL ORIENTATIONS

"Generally, religious organizations start out with a goal orientation, deteriorate to a task orientation, and finally degenerate to the bottom — to control orientation."

I now wish to draw your attention to something that is foundational to management. There are three basic types of organizational orientation or organizational mentalities.

The Task Mentality

First, there is TASK orientation. Task orientation says, "Do this — do that — do something else." Task orientation is primarily concerned with the performance and activity of the moment, and not with the distant goal. The task mentality is revealed in the following illustration with which I am sure you are all acquainted. A man walked up to several workmen.

He asked one workman, "What are you doing?"
"I'm laying bricks."
He addressed another, "What are you doing?"
"I am installing glass."
Finally, he spoke to a man who was wheeling a wheelbarrow, "What are you doing?"
"I'm building a cathedral."

All of these men except the last had a task orientation. In industry the task orientation expresses itself this way: "Screw on that nut. Never mind what you are building. Just screw that nut on that bolt." The average church or mission has a task orientation. "Here is what we do. Here is the activity in which we are engaged."

The Control Mentality

There is another kind of orientation, control. The control orientation is concerned primarily with government, authority and decisions. Control orientation says the most important thing about our association is to make sure that control is maintained, that a proper form of government is perpetuated, and that we do things to a certain standard. Control says it does not make any difference whether we accomplish anything or not, but let us make sure that we *do it right.*

The Goal Mentality

Then, there is another type of orientation, GOAL orientation. Goal orientation says, government, authority, procedure, precedent, history, all must serve an accomplishment. Goal orientation says, everything that is done (task) must strategically contribute to the stated goal. Goal orientation is obsessed with clearly defined objectives. Everything else is subservient to the objective. This is the hardest orientation to maintain. Generally, religious organizations start out with a goal orientation, deteriorate to a task orientation, and finally degenerate to the bottom — to control orientation.

I have been talking about evangelical ecumenicity for a long time and have been exercised about ecumenicity within a predetermined theological framework. One day I was talking with a lady about her mission. She was the head of a small but prominent mission. But, they had not had a new missionary in eight years and they were deteriorating. They were not growing in any way and yet they were perpetuating their old structures. They had degenerated to the bottom, to the control pattern. I said to her, "Dear lady, why don't you merge your mission with somebody that can bring vitality and help in the areas where you need it so that the people involved in your work can accomplish the goals to which they originally committed themselves?" "Oh, merge! We could not merge. That would be an invasion of the sanctity of the origin of our mission." What she was really saying was, "We have no goal other than the perpetuation of our form." Perpetuate she will, and sadly enough so will her constituency!

It is very easy to substitute sentiment for organizational purpose. It is a fierce battle. Our job, in part, is to lead our followers back to a goal orientation.

Is this Biblical? Yes, indeed — "Forgetting those things which are behind and reaching forth unto those things which are before, I press toward the mark for the prize of the high calling of God in Christ Jesus" (Phil. 3:13,14). "What mean ye to weep and break my heart? For I am ready not to be bound only, but also to die at Jerusalem for the name of the Lord Jesus" (Acts 21:13). "I'm ready to preach" (Rom. 1:15). "He steadfastly set his face to go to Jerusalem" (Luke 9:51). It is very Biblical. I may only lay bricks with one hand and wield a sword with the other, but I am going to build the wall.

It is our spiritual degeneration that has taken us down this bitter road to task and control orientation to the exclusion of our goal orientation. Some of us in our organizations will have a bitter struggle to ever regain a goal orientation. Sometimes it cannot be regained in an organization. Maybe you have heard of the inevitable cycle in religious organizations. It starts with a *man* with a vision and a burden. Thus it becomes a *movement,* and this generally degenerates into a *machine.* Then, finally, it becomes a *monument.* These are the four "M's" of organizational deterioration and it results in "control organization." This mentality says in effect, "Never mind whether we are doing anything; let us just make sure that we are doing it properly!"

The best way we have discovered to get things done through a group of people committed to a common objective is to have someone within the group doing the work of planning, leading, organizing and controlling.

Two Principles

The *principle of ministry priority.* This principle teaches us that when we are called upon to perform both management and ministry work during the same period, we tend to give first priority to ministry work. Now, let me illustrate. Here you have a group of church planters, evangelists, in a given situation, country or province. These people, however few or many, are banded together to do church-planting. The purpose of this organization is to evangelize with the view to establishing local groups of believers in this province or city. One of these men is put in the position of chairman, manager, superintendent, director or whatever you want to call him. This man will plan, lead, organize and control in behalf of these people. Ministry work is preaching, evangelizing, conducting meetings, visiting, handing out literature, making disciples, etc. Now, when this man who is skilled in ministry is put in a managerial position, and is required to both minister and manage at the same time, he will tend to give preference to ministry rather than to managing.

It is important to understand the difference between ministry and managing. This principle could apply to a machine shop where you have three men operating pieces of machinery. One of them is made the manager, but he is also required to operate a machine at the same time. He will tend to let the work of management slip in deference to the operating work every time.

You and I are put in positions of management. Our constant temptation is to minister rather than to manage. We will always sermonize. We will always go out and meet people and talk with people. We will do anything before we manage. And this is disastrous in its final results because it throws the group into chaos and confusion. You meet these symptoms when a man who should be managing is exclusively ministering. People commonly say, "Well, I don't know what we are here for — I don't know what he is doing." People will constantly hold the other people in suspicion with respect to their activities and motives when there is lack of management. Lack of management leads to frustration and results in people casting their minds back to the "good old days when there was just Joe and Bill and me out here and we knew what we were doing. But it is all changed now." The cause is a lack of management.

The principle of *organizational levels* teaches us that the lower the organizational level, the more ministry work a manager is able to perform. Now, conversely, the higher the organizational level, the more a man is required to manage. I

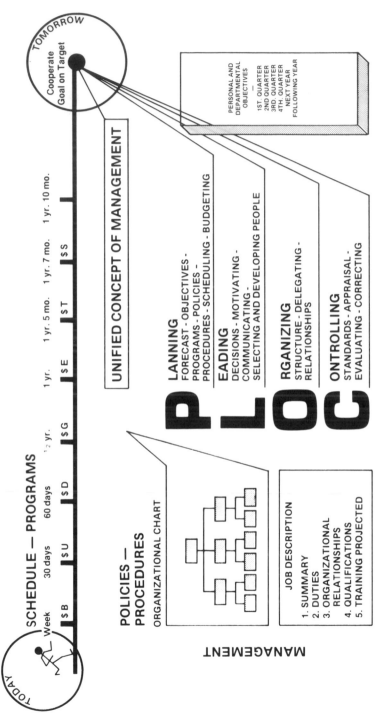

UNIFIED CONCEPT OF MANAGEMENT

P LANNING
FORECAST - OBJECTIVES -
PROGRAMS - POLICIES -
PROCEDURES - SCHEDULING - BUDGETING

L EADING
DECISIONS - MOTIVATING -
COMMUNICATING -
SELECTING AND DEVELOPING PEOPLE

O RGANIZING
STRUCTURE - DELEGATING -
RELATIONSHIPS

C ONTROLLING
STANDARDS - APPRAISAL -
EVALUATING - CORRECTING

SCHEDULE — PROGRAMS

Week   30 days   60 days   ½ yr.   1 yr.   1 yr. 5 mo.   1 yr. 7 mo.   1 yr. 10 mo.

$ B $ U $ D $ G $ E $ T $ S

TODAY

TOMORROW
Cooperate
Goal on Target

PERSONAL AND
DEPARTMENTAL
OBJECTIVES

1ST. QUARTER
2ND QUARTER
3RD QUARTER
4TH. QUARTER
NEXT YEAR
FOLLOWING YEAR

POLICIES —
PROCEDURES

ORGANIZATIONAL CHART

JOB DESCRIPTION

1. SUMMARY
2. DUTIES
3. ORGANIZATIONAL
   RELATIONSHIPS
4. QUALIFICATIONS
5. TRAINING PROJECTED

MANAGEMENT

do not think this needs any enlargement. Where you are determines how much of your time should be spent in planning, leading, organizing and controlling. It is very interesting, though, to note that the Christian world at large is not quite ready to accept management as work. We accept it as a reward for faithfulness or stature or achievement, but do not see it as work.

Because we are not geared in our mentality to accept management as a type of work for Christian organization, we do not require people to have training in this sphere. We do not set people aside and say, "Your job is to plan, lead, organize and control."

What if you hired a person to paint your house and he came with ladders, paint, and paint brushes and sat down and said, "Well, it needs painting all right, but I think I will drink some coffee." And he drank coffee for four hours. Then he said, "That house sure needs painting and I know I ought to paint it. Somebody has to paint it, but I think I will work in the garden. I like flowers."

Well, this could be stretched on and on. The point is, he is not doing what he is supposed to do. We will try to discover as we go along why we avoid management work.

CHAPTER 4
DEVISE THE PLANS
Planning —
Its Characteristics and Principles

PLANNING — ITS CHARACTERISTICS AND PRINCIPLES

"Informed planning is based upon the fact that phenomena do not occur singly. Everything comes preceded by many other things, accompanied by many things and followed by many things. The cause-and-effect relationship of things is the most important natural law we have. Planning, therefore, is doing specified work today to cause desired results tomorrow."

Louis A. Allen in *The Management Profession* defines planning as, "The work a manager performs to pre-determine a course of action." According to him, the all-encompassing view of planning includes the following:

1. *Forecasting:* The work a manager performs to estimate the future.

2. *Establishing objectives:* The work a manager performs to determine the end results to be accomplished with the people involved.

3. *Programming:* The work a manager performs to establish the sequence and priority of action-steps to be followed in reaching objectives.

4. *Scheduling:* The work a manager performs to establish a time sequence for program steps.

5. *Budgeting:* The work a manager performs to allocate resources necessary to accomplish objectives.

6. *Procedure:* The work a manager performs to develop and apply standardized methods of performing specific work.

7. *Policies:* The work a manager performs to develop and interpret standing decisions that apply to recurrent questions and problems of significance to the enterprise as a whole.

What all this says is that planning is one of the most important words in the management functions. Always vital in successful management, planning has assumed unparalleled importance in these days of jet-swift change. Abraham Lincoln said in 1858, "If we could first know where we are, and whither we are tending, we could better judge what to do and how to do it." Informed planning is based upon the fact that phenomena do not occur singly. Everything comes preceded by many other things. The cause-and-effect relationship of things is the most important natural law we have. Planning, therefore, is doing specified work today to cause desired results tomorrow.

Planning is Difficult

Why do we have such difficulty with planning? A Vice-President of Westinghouse Company said, "Today the world is changing so rapidly that we cannot train to meet a given situation. We must educate people to cope with whatever changes may occur." Here is where we have failed in Christian work. We have trained pastors to meet issues that we faced fifteen years ago. Those battles have been fought. Now, we must educate people to cope with whatever changes may occur in the future, and there are only three things about the future, that we are certain of:

1. The future will not be like the past.
2. The future will not be like we think it is going to be.
3. The rate of change will be faster than ever before.

Look again so that you can see all the components of planning. These things all fit together like a piece of fine machinery. You can take them out and examine them one at a time, but in order for a plan to work all of the things have to fit together like a piece of machinery. There are seven of them listed above.

Decisions Made In Advance

With these seven parts of planning in mind, I want first to consider the characteristics of planning. The first characteristic is that planning consists of decisions made in advance of action. Are you aware how difficult decision-making is for the average human being? I saw a cartoon some time ago. A girl was speeding along the road in her car and she came to a fork in the road. There was a sign in the island in the middle of the diverging roads that said, "Take either road." She ran into the post in the middle. As she climbed out of the car and spoke to the policeman the caption read, "I couldn't make up my mind which one to take."

Indecisiveness is one of the greatest enemies of management. Somebody comes into my office and says, "I would like to talk to you about our work, our organization. We cannot get decisions. Nobody wants to decide. Everybody seeks to avoid responsibility." Often the person will say, "We have to write to New York, Chicago, London or to somewhere else to get a decision, and this demoralizes people terribly."

Planning is difficult because planning says, "Today we are deciding many issues related to the future." Planning involves decisions made in advance of action. Nothing so reveals courage and direction on the part of a Christian worker like serious planning. We are certain of what God wants us to accomplish. We are committed under the direction of the Holy Spirit to a certain thing. These are the decisions necessary to move in this direction. If you fire a bullet towards a bull's-eye, it is very difficult to catch up with it and change its course. Actually, we would often prefer to be without purpose to the choice of purpose that commits us in a definite direction. Today's purposes, aims, and decisions commit us tomorrow, and next month, and next year.

The Behavior of People

The second characteristic of planning is that it deals with future *behavior of people*. Do not assume that the people you deal with are any different than the people that anyone else deals with in the world, in industry, in business or in another country.

A man asked me after I had been in Africa about a day and a half, "What are your impressions about Africa?" "Well," I said, "I have none yet except that it it like every other place I have ever been in. It is full of people!"

As trite as this sounds people are an amazingly common denominator. In these past few years, as I have travelled and observed missions in many situations and have met missionaries who come from all over the world, I have been amazed. As you talk to them you can narrow the problems down to a small list. They are basically the same in every country, and the greatest problem is: "We deal with people." You must not say, "Well, it is different in industry." No, it is precisely the same. I have gone to industrial management seminars. I have listened to these men in industrial settings grapple with the same problems that you and I are grappling with in our work. They ask precisely the same questions you ask. When we plan, we are deciding now that other people will carry out specified actions at future periods. This means we have to coordinate, motivate, channel, guide and communicate without fail.

One of the most important things we can learn about the future behavior of people is found in a catchy phrase that I want to leave with you: *take people action*. The principle is, if you expect someone to co-operate with you later in doing something, involve them now in the decision to do it. Two of the most important aspects of planning, dealing with the future behavior of people, are these: conditioning and timing.

We must condition people! Remember, management on the part of the Christian worker is never a partner to subterfuge or insincerity or anything that is the slightest bit dishonest or misrepresentative. Never! Conditioning does not mean deceiving a person or hood-winking him or pulling the wool over his eyes. Conditioning means giving the person information so that he knows the facts. It means involving him in everything that you know about the situation.

People hate secretiveness on the part of a leader. Why is a man secretive? Because his ego craves to know something that somebody else does not know.

R.E. Thompson, Chairman of the Board of the Far Eastern Gospel Crusade for many years, founder of Missionary

Internship, and a missionary to China, says, ''Tell your people everything you can tell them and they will seldom demand that you tell them what you should not tell them. There is a place for secrets, but if you will tell your people all you can, you will seldom find them asking you to tell them what you should not tell them.''

How you go about telling depends upon the subject matter and the situation at hand. Some things can be adequately conveyed in a memorandum or a letter, but letters are poor vehicles for communication! The best way, of course, is face to face; but the larger the group the bigger the problem. The leader should take advantage of every opportunity with his people to condition them, and if you faithfully condition people, they will not hold it against you when you have forgotten. One of the manager's jobs is to condition people for the inevitable change that is coming down the road. God revealed His ways to Moses and His acts to the children of Israel. The man at the top must constantly be conditioning the people under him. Take every opportunity and do it every way you can.

The other aspect of dealing with the behavior of people is *timing*. There is a time question -- When? The immature leader always feels he has got to do it now; and if he finds he cannot do it now, he takes it as a personal affront. That is immaturity. I remember one time as a pastor I had a bright idea. The only problem was that it occurred to me on Monday and we were having our annual business meeting on Wednesday. So, I sprung it on the congregation! Do you know what happened? They threw it out. Because it was a bad idea? No, it was a good one. A year later they accepted the idea with no problem. What was wrong? My timing was off. When we are planning for the future behavior of people, we have to have both condition and time. This means that you must know well in advance definitely where you are going.

The Role of Change

The third characteristic is that planning involves *change*. I am convinced that change is the most evident characteristic of our time and I am also convinced that the average Christian worker is oblivious to it. Some of us are living as if conditions were the same today that prevailed twenty-five years ago. We are as out of touch as we can be. We are not aware of the changes that have developed around us. American Management Association President, Lawrence Appley, in trying to describe how rapidly changes are taking place, put it this way: "We are confronted with the rate of change -- it is the rate of change of change." It is no longer the rate of change -- it is the rate of change of change! Alvin Toffler's best selling book, *Future Shock*, discusses this at great length. Very rapidly change is taking place and it is touching you and the people you are working with. You might occasionally think, "Oh, I am living in a city or village where change will not affect us." Don't believe it. Technology has advanced more in the last fifty years than in the preceding five thousand years and in the next five years we will double our technological advance. Very few Christian workers are able to adapt to the demands of this kind of change in society.

Consider for a moment the following. More people are alive on the earth today than had died since mankind first appeared. Some experts are predicting that by the year 2,000 we will have instant world-wide television communication. Many of the countries of the world will proudly display automated highways. These are already in the experimental stages. Fish will be herded and raised in off-shore pens in the ocean to feed the population. There will be automatic atomic and hydrogen controls. Drugs will alter basic personality patterns in the individual. Eric Hoffer in his book, *The Ordeal of Change*, says, "Nobody really likes the new. We all fight change. Taking a new step, uttering a new word, is what people fear the most." And for people like you and me, the issue is *change or die*.

In 1960 the Gallup Poll in the United States revealed that 14% of the population felt that the church in America was irrelevant and unrelated to real life situations. In 1967, the same poll showed that 54% of the population said the church was unrelated to society. We are being pressed in a corner these days to see if we are really going to adapt to meet the needs of a changing world.

I was conducting a week of meetings in a seaside town where people come in large crowds during the summer. They stay in hotels and tourist homes and swim in the ocean all day. I was preaching in a very conservative church. An innovative evangelistic group was having meetings there. They had about 60-70 students working through the summer trying to evangelize the young drop-out crowd. I was invited to observe their efforts, so I said to myself, "I'm going to work with these people." After the service I tried to look contemporary. I took my tie off and pulled my shirt tail out and looked as sloppy as I could. I would slouch down the street and go to what they called their "Hunger Hanger" -- the place where they had psychedelic posters on the windows and walls. Well, I had the time of my life.

I found a whole segment of the population that rejected the Church. One night two of these fellows walked into the church where I was preaching at the end of the meeting with their scruffy beards, smoking cigarettes and smelling unpleasantly! You could have heard a pin drop. The people were standing around in their nice clothes, staring at them. "What are they doing here?" Well, I knew the fellows, so I went to the back of the church and greeted them. "Hello, how are you?" I shook hands with them and everybody stared dumbfoundedly. "What's going on? Who are they?" Do you know who they are? They are representatives of a great segment of this world, which we need to adapt to so that we can win them to Christ.

Someone once said, "Difficulties result when attachments, proper to faith, are transferred uncritically to methods of work." It is our ideological dogmatism, our theoretically unsupported assertions, that get us into trouble. We think that because something worked in the past, it is going to work in the present. But it might not work in our day at all. It depends upon whether our emphasis is task, control or goal. That is what makes the difference.

Emerson lamented, "Improved means to unimproved ends." Einstein concurred: "Few things so characterize our day as perfection of means and confusion of goals." That is the world. The world often perfects and improves means to uncertain or less than noble ends; the church pursues noble ends, but with antiquated means. Change! Change anything, change everything that can be changed to accomplish our goal. Now does, this mean we change our theology? No! I am not suggesting that. I am saying that in our planning we should come up with such a commitment to a goal that we consider everything, old and new, in the light of achieving that goal.

Why do we not make the effort that is required to establish objectives, estimate the future program, establish budgets and procedures? What are the barriers to this planning? Let me suggest that the first reason is simply that *we do not know how.* Some of us do not plan because *we have never seen it done.*

Secondly, we do not plan because *most of us prefer to do things than to think about them.* Planning is thinking. Planning is coordinating. Planning is analyzing. Planning is communicating. Planning is inter-acting. Planning is revising, appraising, criticizing, and it is easier to do it than it is to think about it.

Thirdly, the barrier to planning is *the uncertainty of the future.* We do not know what tomorrow is going to be like. So we tend just to say, "Oh, what is the use? Every time I make plans they go astray. So I am just not going to try to plan any more." That is limited perspective and it reveals a task-orientation rather than goal-orientation. Goal-orientation will continually say, "Here is the thing we are committed to achieve." We have to keep revising and regrouping and bringing pressures to bear so that all of the activities aim toward the goal.

As we proceed in the actual planning process there are six principles that need to be kept In mind.

Present Choice

Principle number one: *the principle of present choice* teaches us that current decisions limit future action. What does this mean? Let us suppose that our missionary organization is about to go into a certain country or a certain province and the goal in this endeavor is church planting. As we become more definite we say that within five years we want churches started in the population centers. Within ten years, a specific number of churches in these particular locations.

Now, we are agreed. We are entering this new area. There is mutual commitment that this is our goal, but after we get in there we find that these poor people do not know how to read and write. Are we going to have some literacy work? Then we find that these people are ill. Are we going to have some medical work? Then after a while we find that these people are hungry. They need some aid in agricultural development. Are we going to have some agricultural missionaries come in? Are we going to predetermine our goal in advance or are we to proliferate our activities after we are in, oftentimes to the weakening of all our purposes? What determines our goals? Is it need?

A missionary in children's work had a classic example of this problem. She was working alongside two or three couples in an area in Japan, and soon after she became involved in the children's work she found that in the wintertime all the children coming to the meetings had runny noses. So she would wipe their noses. Well, she found that all she was doing was wiping noses! Finally, she decided, ''My goal is not to see that they have clean noses. My goal in these limited thirty or forty minutes that I have these children is to teach them something they will never forget from the Word of God.'' So she let their noses drip!

What determines what we are going to do? Necessity? Or are we going to make decisions now that will limit future action? This is why planning is difficult. Once we get into the thing we will find many other noble purposes which may or may not be of God. The fact that they are noble, the fact that they are needful activities, does not necessarily mean that we are qualified to get involved in them. Sometimes we proliferate our activities to the weakening of our main purposes. In planning we have to determine in advance.

Positive Action

Principle number two: *the principle of positive action* teaches us that the probability of a future event occurring increases as effort is applied systematically toward its realization. We have X number of people, X number of hours, and X amount of money. Our resources are limited, and we must not have them dissipated. This is why you must say, ''We want a ditch dug from A to B'' instead of, ''All right. All of you as you feel led, dig the ditch.''

We must have a goal commitment, a goal understanding, that forces us to be drawn together in its completion. I see this from the missionary's point of view and the pastor's point of view. This is a never-ending problem. The pastor or missionary says his job is church planting or evangelizing. Then he finds that there are myriads of other activities he is pressured into, to the exclusion of the thing he preaches and talks about. The point is, we ought to be so oriented to the goal that we will critically evaluate these other pressing needs.

I find that most Christian organizations are so diversified in their activities that they are ineffective in everything. We have an exaggerated concept about our abilities and resources and an undisciplined approach to our task. One mission executive put down in his goals for his organization: "Our goal is to evangelize the whole world." What an exaggerated concept of his abilities and resources!

Commensurate Effort

Principle number three: *the principle of commensurate effort.* This teaches us that effort applied should be commensurate with or proportionate to the results desired. If we could just grasp hold of that one thing, what a difference it could make in our ministry. But again, it presupposes an identity of goal and a commitment to that goal. It critically looks at everything you are doing and says, Here is the goal to which I am committing myself. But we are so subjective that we have great difficulty evaluating this sort of thing critically.

Planning Stability

Principle number four: *the principle of planning stability.* This teaches us that the stability of a plan tends to vary inversely with its extension. This means that I can plan very accurately for a week, with less accuracy for a month, with even less accuracy for a year, and with even less accuracy as the time is extended even further. What does this mean in regard to planning? Does it mean that because of the instability of the lengthening of the plan, that I should not plan? No, it makes planning all the more imperative. Also, it means that I will constantly up-date my plan. Planning is a continuing work.

Potential Resistance

Principle number five: *the greater the departure of planned changes from present ways, the greater the potential resistance by the people involved.* Do you know who resists change? You and I resist change. And it is perhaps true that the older we are the more we resist it, but this is not necessarily true. The more insecure we are, the more we resist change. Provincialism contributes to resistance to change. We have to anticipate resistance to change and we cannot scold our people when they resist change. Some pastors I have talked to do not have a good word to say for their congregation in this area -- ''These people resist everything that is new and innovative.'' Let us appreciate the fact that we also resist change, that we do not want someone coming in and imposing something new upon us. If we realize this about ourselves it will help us to realize it about other people.

Future Events

Now in the sixth place, *future events tend to result from current and past occurrences.* Organizations are what they have been becoming. We determine tomorrow to the extent that we identify clearly what we want to accomplish and apply efforts today to bring it to pass. This is present diligence with clearly defined tomorrow mindedness.

CHAPTER 5
IDENTIFY THE GOALS
The Establishing of Objectives

THE ESTABLISHING OF OBJECTIVES

"I am not concerned with what your objectives are, but I am concerned that you know what they are and that people with whom you work know what they are."

Now we turn our attention to one of the very important components of planning. In a previous chapter we defined the various components of planning, beginning with the work of estimating the future and going down through programs, policies, budgets, schedules, etc. One of the most important aspects of planning -- in fact, a component completely inseparable from the very concept of planning -- is the establishing of objectives. We must understand what our objectives are. We must be able to articulate them. They must be in written form. They must be widely displayed. People must have access to them. The people within our organization must be committed to them. In short, everyone in our organization must *know* what the objectives are.

To a very large degree, the effectiveness of our corporate efforts in any human enterprise depends upon our ability to concisely articulate our objectives, and the degree to which we are corporately enthusiastic about these objectives. In international organizations and operations, like missions, we get into all kinds of trouble. A frequent complaint I have heard from new missionaries and from older ones that can remember the frustrations of their earlier years is, ''I am not doing what I came out here to do. I am not engaged in the kind of work that was described to me when I was in seminary.'' I know the arguments. But still there is this basic frustration. On the one hand we visualize our purposes as one thing and then when we get to our field of service we find that we are involved in something altogether different. At that point we rationalize: ''Well, look Olan, you've got to do what the Lord leads you to do.''

The problem really is one of not knowing what our objectives are. Frequently when you talk to people from the same organization, you get two or more sets of answers for the same question. I am not concerned with what your objectives are, but I am concerned that you know what they are and that people with whom you work know what they are. I am concerned that everything possible be directed toward the accomplishing of those objectives, regardless of what they are.

I came upon a very interesting article in a daily devotional magazine some time ago that speaks eloquently on this subject of objectives. A newly-hired traveling salesman wrote his first report to the home office. It stunned the executives in the sales department because it was obvious that the ''new help'' was completely illiterate. This is what he wrote: ''I seen this outfit which they never bought a dime's worth of nothin' from us and I sole them some goods. I am now going to Chicawgo.'' Before the services of the ignorant man could be terminated by the sales manager, this letter came from Chicago, ''I cum here and sole them haff a millyon.'' Fearful if he did and afraid if he did not fire the man, the sales manager dumped the problem in the lap of the president. The following morning the executives and office personnel were amazed to see a memo from the president posted on the bulletin board with the two letters written by the ignorant salesman. It read like this: "We've ben spendin' two much time tryin' to spel instead of tryin' to sel. Let's watch those sails. I want everybody should read these letters from Gootch who is on the rode doin' a grate job for us and you should go out and do like he done." We should find out what we are supposed to do, and then do it.

One day I was showing a visitor around a church which had about 2,000 people in attendance. It was pastored by a friend of mine and had the oddest kind of arrangement you would ever want to see. I was showing this fellow around and explaining how this works and how that works. It is the most unconventional set-up, and my friend quickly spotted that and said, "Somebody ought to tell this pastor that this will not work." Well, the only problem was, it did work. This pastor was accomplishing his objectives.

Earlier I said that everything should be directed toward the accomplishment of our objectives. Our organizational structure should lend itself relentlessly to the accomplishment of those objectives. Our policies should contribute to the accomplishment of those objectives. Precedent and what we learn from history should dictate to us how to accomplish our objectives. But our problem most of the time is that we do not really know what our objectives are.

Objective Questions

Lorne Sanny, the successor to Dawson Trotman in the Navigator movement, is a sharp and creative manager. He was not always so. After his succession to the leadership, Lorne went through a very difficult period, and it was only after he came upon a little booklet entitled *Management*, written by the President of the National Bank of Detroit, that he began to see that here were some skills that he could acquire. After studying the subject of management for a number of years, Lorne Sanny came up with four questions relative to objectives. He came upon these questions because he found that he had to have some point of contact with the people who were serving under him. These four questions are four of the most perceptive objective-oriented questions I have ever seen.

Sanny says, "There are four things I always ask people who report to me. First, I want to know plainly, *"What are your objectives?"* You start working on this and it will revolutionize your life. Ask this question about the next sermon you are going to preach. What are my objectives in delivering this sermon? What are my objectives in having this business meeting? What are my objectives in having this interview with this person?

His second question is -- *what are your opportunities* or what are your open doors? Often opportunities can be made, often they cannot. We must be perceptive enough to know what doors are open. A lot of time can be wasted waiting idly for doors to open and energy can be wasted trying to open doors that simply can't be opened.

His third question is, *what are your resources?* Here we must be realistic, not mystical. Do not spiritualize where God demands a practical outlook. Do not become spiritually evasive where God demands pragmatism. What are my resources? How many men have I got? How many hours have I got? How much money have I got? How many cars have I got? How many Bibles have I got? How much literature have I got?

The fourth question has to do with strategy and then it reviews the list from the bottom to the top. *What is your strategy for applying your resources to your opportunities to obtain your objectives?* This will force a man to think creatively. This removes the responsibility from the manager to devise all the steps to be taken, and thrusts the creative responsibility upon the individuals themselves.

The Power of Goals

Goals have a powerful effect. Objectives clearly articulated and mutually agreed upon in a group have a powerful effect. This more than anything else explains the supreme accomplishments of new organizations. New organizations often emerge and accomplish a great deal in a short period of time. Probably some of you reminisce about the old days of your church or organization when you accomplished so much. Of course, we tend to distort the past. We tend to remember only the good about the past and forget the bad. Someone has said:

"There are only two good places to be: the place where you have just been and the place where you are going." We normally can only look realistically at the moment, but nonetheless it is a fact that new organizations are highly goal-oriented or objective-oriented and everything is subservient to the goal.

This need not be exclusively a characteristic of the new or recently-emerged organization. It can be a continuing characteristic of any organization if we want it to be and if we are willing to make it so at all costs.

Let us see the powerful effect of clear objectives. Most good work in management is problem-oriented; that is, it aims at accomplishing some specific end, some goal, or it aims at achieving some terminal point. The definition of these objectives for the whole organization, for all subordinate organizations, and for individuals in it, is the logical starting place for management improvement. This is important. Many old, staid, ponderous, slow-moving churches and Christian organizations can be rejuvenated to a goal orientation. Many cannot. If it is possible, then it is so only as we make an attack on this subject of objectives. I hope you do not think I am belaboring the point. I have observed that every book you read on the subject of management says the same thing. This is where we have to start: the objectives for the total organization. Put this in a pyramid form. The top piece would be the objective of the total organization. Everything underneath this, every subordinate organization, must likewise be committed in this direction, though it will have goals all its own. This applies to the individual also. Every individual within this organization must have goals that are incorporated into the main objectives.

Four effects of unclear objectives

1. Unclear objectives lead to unclear methods of operation. The absence of a goal justifies almost any activity espoused by an individual under the guise of, "This is my burden," or "This is my calling," or "This is the Lord's leading." I do not mean to minimize this nor speak lightly of holy things. But I think there is more evasiveness in this than most of us in Christian work are willing to admit, and it is tragic. If you do not have a goal, then any road will get you there.

2. You cannot measure results without some prior expectation against which to judge them. In other words, if you do not have clear objectives, then almost any level or degree or quality of performance will satisfy the people involved. Almost any activity can be justified on an individualistic basis. This is where we are in missions and in our churches.

There are, however, some people who will never work in an organization. If we were able to devise an ideal organization, some people would never fit into it. Let us accommodate these people outside organizational structures. Let us recognize that not everyone can conform to an organizational structure. If there is an individual who must work on his own, let him go! The great bulk of humanity, however, needs the kind of restraining and control provided by an organization.

3. If you are not clear on your objectives, you do not know when things are drifting. You do not realize it until a lifetime has been spent and then, suddenly it dawns upon you, "I didn't achieve it. I didn't hit it." Oh, we rationalize, we exonerate ourselves, we excuse ourselves, we make allowances; but in the end we find we have failed.

4. People in an organization cannot perform with maximum effectiveness if they are unaware of the goals, the purposes of their work, or how well they are doing in relation to the goals.

There are three main problems in managing Christian workers. They are uncertainty of the job, how am I doing, and where do I go for help? I have talked with scores of missionaries who have spent a term on the field and have not known until they were ready to go home and had a pre-furlough interview how they were doing! One reason we fail to tell people how they are doing is that some of us in responsible positions are insecure ourselves. We have not trusted the Holy Spirit to give us the courage to face a man and tell him how he is doing. People want help. They need help. If we want to have effective management results we will build into our situations ways for people to get help.

"Look, I'm having trouble with my wife and children. Where do I go for help?"

"I'm having problems with the local or national church. Where do I go for help?"

"I'm having problems in my own mind with some theological questions. Where do I get help? Is there a person or a group to which I can go for help?"

A good manager will establish a relationship with his people so that they will gladly come and say, "I need help. Can you tell me what to do?"

In articulating these goals, we prepare ourselves with a very basic foundation for all of our future performance. Goals are not always adhered to with equal enthusiasm by every member of the organization. People deeply committed come in but they become disillusioned and need to be reminded repeatedly of the goals of the organization. We must be re-oriented to the goal week after week, year after year.

The Establishing of Goals

Now the question comes: "How do we establish goals?" First of all, there are two types of goals -- long-range and short-range goals. Normally we think of long-range goals running from five years or more. Anything less than that becomes short-range. How do we go about establishing these goals? This is the hardest work you will ever do. It is easy to write down what you think ought to be done. However, when it involves twenty, thirty, fifty or a hundred people, it is difficult. We start with the ultimate goal. What do we want to accomplish ultimately? For example, this could be to build cathedrals in every metropolitan center in Africa. We must determine what the goal is and then work back toward "today." That is the big job. When obstacles arise, we are tempted to avoid them, and concentrate on other goals -- perhaps an intermediate-range goal. Management is concerned with applying the pressure to get back on course, again heading for the target. You have read how missiles work. The basic function of the guidance system of a rocket is first of all to determine the goal or the target, and then to feed back to the earth at a guidance center or computer the detailed, minute information that will tell the operators of the machinery if it is veering off the slightest bit. In other words, they do not wait to correct it; they act immediately. The missile must be pushed back on course.

That is the concern of management. Management is not concerned with dominating another human personality, nor with asserting itself, nor with the acquiring and attaining of a status. Management is concerned with objectives. This is why you must use management skills.

What happens when you do not use management skills? You veer off the course. Not only that, if you do not use management control, when you veer off, confusion, loss of confidence, and frustration results.

Lack of Management Brings Frustration

The one emotion I observe most in Christian work is frustration. It is not frustration because people are not responding to the gospel and being saved. Any Biblically-oriented person has an answer to that kind of devilish frustration. It is frustration resulting from a lack of management within our human enterprise. I have been in countries where the missionaries are suffering all sorts of hardships. I have been in some of those tribal situations in southeast Asia, in Thailand, in Viet Nam, in Cambodia, where missionaries live in tremendously primitive situations. Some of you have lived and worked there. Missionaries are not frustrated by this. I have seen national pastors working in situations in Cambodia, where they could not hand out a piece of literature without a permit from a police officer. I have known of pastors who have had their wives imprisoned because they allegedly gave out a piece of literature without permission, but these pastors have been absolutely radiant in the face of that kind of persecution. Yet in the face of poor management they have been in absolute bondage and defeat. This could be different if we simply recognized some of these management skills and acquired them.

Rules for Establishing Objectives

Someone has said that there are five rules for establishing objectives. The first is, *consider past performance.* That is to say, know precisely what has been the situation in the past. Records, trends, and honest input from your followers provide you with this background. Second, *set realistic levels*. It is very easy for religious workers to violate this under the guise of faith! Third, *use measurable terms*. This is easiest in relation to income, attendance, concerts, and facilities. It is enormously difficult in areas like learning attitudes, and morale. Fourth, *build in an improvement factor*. People will not long pursue mere ideals that have no rewards. And few rewards have the dynamics of improvement. Fifth, *take people action*. In order to secure the creative cooperation of followers, a leader must provide for participation on their part. This does not imply a necessity for allowing them to vote -- merely participate.

Group Goals vs. Individual Goals

There is another aspect that should be mentioned. That is, the difference between corporate goals -- the total goal of the association of human beings -- and individual goals. There is a distinction. We cannot adequately determine individual goals until we have determined corporate goals. You must have the same relationship between corporate goals and individual goals that you have between long-range and short-range goals. You start with your long-range goals and work back. Likewise you start with your corporate goals and then you begin to work in your departmental goals, your divisional goals, your project goals, your institutional goals and your individual goals. (see p. 58)

Within the pyramid there may be other pyramids. If the goal is the planting of churches in cities in hitherto unreached areas, you may have a large project, e.g. a housing development, and within this you would have another pyramid. Within that pyramid there could be other pyramids, depending upon how large this organization is. Individuals would be related in these situations as well as in the overall picture. All of these activities move toward the ultimate goal. It is this concept that makes the difference between success and failure. A strong natural leader instinctively, by virture of his dynamic personality, accomplishes this sort of thing. In a very natural way, almost totally psychological, he achieves the goal very effectively. But in the absence of such a man the articulation of objectives and the adherence to those objectives can do the same thing.

I hope you see the difference between long-range and short-range goals, between corporate and individual goals. Therefore, let your prime target be the determination of your objectives. What is your group trying to accomplish? Assuming that we have established objectives and that we have satisfactorily taken people action and our people are committed to the stated goals, the next thing to do is to organize for a particular function.

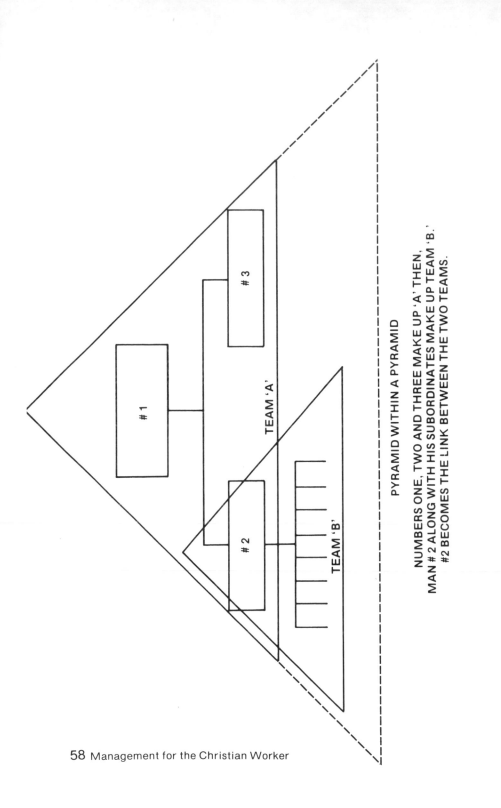

PYRAMID WITHIN A PYRAMID

NUMBERS ONE, TWO AND THREE MAKE UP 'A' THEN,
MAN # 2 ALONG WITH HIS SUBORDINATES MAKE UP TEAM 'B.'
2 BECOMES THE LINK BETWEEN THE TWO TEAMS.

TEAM 'A'

TEAM 'B'

#1

#2

#3

CHAPTER 6
LEARN THE BASICS
Management Organizing Principles

MANAGEMENT ORGANIZING PRINCIPLES

"The criterion by which we measure organizational normality is the achievement of goals. Briefly and succinctly, the implications of organizational dynamics are growth, development and maturity."

In a recent issue of *U.S. News and World Report* there was an interesting story about a British military team trying to cut down on the manpower used in handling a field cannon. Always there had been six men assigned to each cannon but there were only five jobs. The men studied each job as described in the instruction manual. From the first edition on, every manual called for a crew of six. Finally, they located the man who had written the manual originally, a retired general, and they asked him what the sixth man was supposed to do. He replied, "The sixth man? He holds the horses." They had not used horses for many, many years, but the job persisted. No reason was necessary; precedent had become reason enough!

If our objective is clearly defined and if we are convinced that it is of God and are committed to it, the people involved in the organization will accept it as God's assignment. It is then necessary to devise an organizational structure which contributes to achieving of the objectives.

A Definition of Organizing

First, a definition of management organizing. *It is the grouping, the arranging and the relating of the work to be performed, necessary for a group of people to accomplish the goal effectively.* The little blocks in the typical organizational chart do not represent status nor salary levels. They identify and relate work which is necessary in order to accomplish the organizational goals.

A manager must develop an organization capable of accomplishing its objectives. Often alteration of the structure becomes necessary. What things might happen which would indicate the need for alteration of the structure? A change of goal, or the capacities of the people involved, or the environment in which we are trying to accomplish this goal might require such a change. All these may affect the organizational structures. Twenty-five years or so ago in the United States Sunday evening services became very popular. This was a way to reach the unconverted. People often did not have anywhere else to go so they went to church on Sunday night. They did not go Sunday morning because they slept in. They did not have television to watch nor have as many cars then as they do now. But things have changed. If you get any unconverted people into a church today it is on Sunday morning, certainly not on Sunday night. Yet how many churches doggedly persist in having a Sunday evening evangelistic service? We refuse to accept the changes dictated by an evolution in our environment. We have task and tradition orientation!

Alvin Brown says, "Organization defines the part which each member of an enterprise is expected to perform and the relations between such members to the end that their concerted effort or endeavor shall be most effective for the purpose of the enterprise."

Mooney and Riley describe organization as "the form of every human association for the attainment of a common purpose."

General Food Corporation defines organization as, "the plan by which a group of people pool their efforts toward designated objectives through definition and division of activities, responsibilities and authority." Why do we give a man a specific job and give him specific authority and allow him to make specific kinds of decisions? Because that is the best way to accomplish the goal!

The Implication of Organizational Dynamics

Secondly, the implication of organizational dynamics. The simple fact is that organizations are made up of people. People change, environments change, the demands upon an organization are changing from day to day. This means that the people within the organization must be willing to have their structure and their activities altered to accomplish the goal. The organization, like a human being, must evolve. I am sure that you have used as an illustration of spiritual development the tragedy of a physically under-developed person. Some years ago I saw one of the most heart-rending things I have ever seen in my life -- a boy in his teens chronologically who was mentally two years of age. He was almost a vegetable. What a tragedy! Well, this occurs organizationally too. Where organizations are brought into existence, operate effectively for a short time, only to degenerate while their environment moves on ahead of them and they just stay bogged down and entangled and do not develop. Organizations must live and breathe, develop and grow and change.

A seventeen-year-old boy comes to his father and says, "Dad, may I borrow the car tonight?" And his mother says, "Oh, my baby, my baby, my baby...." The father tells her, "My dear, he's no baby. Look at him! He's a six footer." But she has a difficult time thinking of her son as anything but Mama's baby. In the physical development of a person the criterion by which we measure normality is the relationship of that individual to others. However, the criterion by which we measure organizational normality is the achievement of goals. Briefly and succinctly, the implications of organizational dynamics are growth, development and maturity.

In the third place, there is purpose versus sentiment in Christian organizations. In the business world not all businesses are successful and well organized. It would amaze you to know how many people in business study management but go away and never do anything about it. However, business has one advantage that we do not have in Christian work -- what we call a profit and loss statement. If a business does not show a profit, and if over a long period it continues to show a loss, somebody complains -- usually the stockholders. Why? They want a return on their investment. Not only do they want a return on their investment, they want protection for their capital and the greatest protection of that capital is the continuing functioning of that organization to accomplish its goals. They want to make money on the money they have invested. If they do not see this happening on the profit and loss statement regularly, they complain loudly. But unfortunately, we do not have this in Christian work.

We can sink into unbelievable organizational ineffectiveness in Christian work and few will say anything. If complaints are made they are not spoken loudly, or else somebody cries, "Oh, you're touching the Lord's anointed," or, "You're fighting against God," or, "Didn't God bring this organization into existence?" That is sad. It does not make much sense, but we do it anyway. What is it then that perpetuates the organization? It is sentiment.

We had a very serious situation in a church in which I once served. In fact, it was the most serious situation I have ever been confronted with in my ministerial career. A well-meaning but sticky sentimentalist said in a deacon's meeting one night when we were discussing the problem, "Friends, my advice is not to touch the situation. Let's maintain peace." Well, there is a time when silence is not golden: it is yellow cowardice. There is a time when we must sweep aside this kind of peacefulness and sentimentality in order to accomplish our objectives. Do you know that in church, purposefulness is always considered eccentric, always kind of coming at the status quo from the flank? And yet, it is this kind of purposefulness to which God has called us. But, we often find that we prefer to perpetuate the form on the basis of sentiment rather than to insist upon accomplishing our purpose.

Some of us may be so bogged down in sentiment that our church or organization does not have a chance for renewal and adaptation to the accomplishing of our purpose. If that is the case, it is tragic! Our donors or church members do not help. They feed the evil root of sentimentality rather than holding us to the highest and saying: "Are you sure that what you are doing is essential? Can you justify your being there?" Your members will not say that. They will pat you on the head and give you another love offering. An awesome responsibility rests upon us to evaluate ourselves and to develop a goal orientation.

You probably have noticed on the management outline (page 16) that the four major functions of management according to Allen have listed under them all of the activities that apply to those major headings. For example, under management organizing are the activities of organizing; also, the developing of the structure, the maintaining of relationships, and delgation. Let us look at some management organizing principles which relate to organizing as a whole, to the developing of the structure, to the work of delegation and to the work of establishing and maintaining relationships.

1. *The principle of the objective.* The organizational structure should be designed to accomplish established objectives. It follows from this that when the organizational structure no longer accomplishes objectives, you discard it, alter it, or subject it to whatever is necessary in order to accomplish the objectives.

2. *The principle of specialization.* The work assigned to individuals should be specialized insofar as it is consistent with effective human effort. This is the genius of the assembly line. Specialization applies not only to assembly line situations but to managerial situations as well. The more specialized we can make the work, the more skilled the person is apt to become in that work and the more effective he is apt to be over a lengthy period.

Some time ago I was consulted regarding a situation where a woman was assigned to counselling and to bookkeeping. You cannot imagine two more opposite types of work -- counselling and bookkeeping. The woman was terribly frustrated because she was at an age in her life when she was concerned about her own accomplishments. Usually, people at about forty tend to panic. "What have I done? What am I achieving?" Between the ages of forty and forty-five, people often make drastic changes in their vocations under the panic pressure of accomplishment. Her problem was that she was not excelling in either field. With a bit of pressure she was relieved of the bookkeeping and moved into counselling (which she preferred), and she developed an attitude which was much more wholesome.

3. *The principle of management emphasis.* When called upon to supervise two more differing types of work, a manager tends to show preferential emphasis in his decisions and choices. These preferences will be determined primarily by his previous relationships or activities. This can be good or bad, depending upon the needs of the situation.

4. *The principle of maximum span.* A manager should oversee the maximum number of people he can effectively manage. This is assuming that we view management as a type of work to be performed and we recognize it as a legitimate assignment. The number depends upon a variety of things. First, upon the capacity of the manager. Some people have a greater capacity than others. It depends secondly upon the type of work that the people are doing. You can obviously oversee more ditch-diggers than you can research scientists. In the third place, it depends upon geography or dispersal of personnel.

I was involved in a situation where one man was responsible for eighteen men stretched all the way across the United States and Canada. This is an impossible situation. There are not enough days in the week, there are not enough airplanes flying, and if there were the planes, he does not have the energy to relate to that many men spread over that wide an area. So it depends upon capacity; it depends upon the type of work; and it depends upon geography or the dispersal of the people that are being supervised. However, all of that being considered, the manager should manage as many people as he can effectively.

5. *The principle of minimum levels.* The number of organizational levels should be kept at a minimum. To proliferate the organizational levels is not necessarily to increase the effectiveness of the organization itself. We have levels going down, down, down. Minimize those levels. The more levels you multiply this way, the more difficulties you create. The reason is obvious. It takes time for information and decisions to go from the top to the bottom.

Incidentally, have you ever noticed the instinctive answer to every problem? "We are not getting the work done that we should." The first answer, the easiest answer, the spontaneous answer is, "Let us get more people." *More people does not insure the accomplishment of more work.* It only insures the presence of more people. Sometimes work simplification is the answer, not an increased staff.

6. *The principle of carry-over.* The early characteristics of organization tend to persist in later organizational forms. To put it simply, "You never outlive your past." Some of these earlier characteristics will follow you to the very end. You can make appreciable changes, but the past carries over.

7. *The principle of control limits.* Delegation should proceed only to the limit of effective control. Just as a person can only do so much, so he can only be accountable for so much.

8. *The principle of commensurate authority.* Authority should be delegated commensurate with responsibility.

9. *The principle of complete accountability.* The superior is always accountable for the actions of his subordinates. It is not a very pleasant position, but it is always a necessary position.

10. The principle of single reporting relationships. Each person should be accountable to only one supervisor.

Ten Commandments of Good Organization
There are two kinds of efficiency. One kind is only *apparent* and is produced in organizations through the exercise of mere discipline. This is but an imitation of the second, or true efficiency which springs, as Woodrow Wilson said, from "the spontaneous co-operation of a free people." If you are a manager, no matter how great or small your responsibility, it is your job to create and develop this voluntary co-operation

among the people whom you supervise. For no matter how powerful a combination of money, machines and materials an organization may have, they are dead and sterile without a team of *willing, thinking,* and *articulate* people to guide them.

Here are "Ten Commandments of Good Organization," taken from American Management Association, which I have adapted with a few word changes.

1. Definite and clear-cut responsibilities should be assigned to each person or position. We might know today what our job is, but the situation might change so that tomorrow we do not know. We need adequate supervision so that we can rediscover what our job is when it has evolved.

2. Responsibility should always be coupled with corresponding *authority*.

3. No change should be made in the scope or responsibilities *of a position* without a definite understanding to that effect on the part of all persons concerned.

4. No executive or employee, occupying a *single* position in the organization, should be subject to orders from more than one source. Every person should have only one boss. Where it is necessary for one person to have two or three positions, there should not only be a clear understanding as to who gives him orders with respect to which work, but also what is the time allocation for these positions. Otherwise, he is going to be torn and many people who work for him may well be frustrated because they take orders from so many people.

5. Orders should never be given to subordinates over the head of a responsible executive. The manager tells his foreman what he thinks that a certain subordinate under the foreman should do; the manager does not go directly to the subordinate.

6. Criticisms of subordinates should be made privately, and in no case should a subordinate be criticized in the presence of executives or employees of equal or lower rank.

7. No dispute or difference between executive or employee as to authority or responsibilities should be considered too trivial for prompt and careful attention.

8. Promotions, wage changes, and disciplinary action should

always be approved by the executive immediately superior to the one directly responsible.

9. No executive or employee should ever be required, or expected, to be at the same time an assistant to, and a critic of, another.

10. Any executive whose work is subject to regular inspection should, whenever practicable, be given the assistance and facilities necessary to enable him to maintain an independent check of the quality of his own work. You will find he will be harder on himself than you would be on him if you make that arrangement with him. If a person is working under you, he should be given the assistance and the facilities necessary for him to evaluate how well he is doing. He should be given opportunity to report to you so that there can be not only your appraisal of his work but his appraisal of his work, both coming from the same standard.

Sources of Authority

What are the sources of authority by which a man manages? Here are four:

First, the *authority of competence.* The more competent the other fellow knows you are, the more confident he will be that you know what you are talking about. And, the more likely he will be to follow your orders, requests and suggestions. This does not mean that you can manage a treasurer or bookkeeper only if you yourself are an expert treasurer or bookkeeper. It implies your competency as a manager in general.

Second, the *authority of position.* This gives you the right to tell someone else what to do. This has teeth. If you are elected chairman or director, you have to fill your position. What are the two greatest enemies of leadership? To like and to want to be liked. "I cannot discipline this fellow — I like him. I cannot be too hard on that man — I want him to like me."

My father worked for the International Paper Company in construction work from the time he was nineteen years old until his death. Some time ago he was building a mill at Vicksburg, Mississippi, the largest paper mill in the world. I was visiting there and he was showing me through the new mill. We were riding along in the car, and I said, "Dad, what do your men think of you?"

Dad said, "Huh, I can't talk that way to you; you're a preacher."

I said, "No, I'm really interested. What do your men think about you?"

He puffed on his cigar, looked at me and sort of grinned and said, "Well, I heard a couple of men talking in the room next to me the other day. They didn't know I was in there and one of them said, 'Hendrix? Why that grey-headed old . . . !'"

Dad sucked on his cigar vigorously, and said, "I don't care what they think about me. My job is to build mills, not to make friends."

I thought, "Give me that kind of courage too." Not that ruthlessness but that kind of commitment to a purpose. If you are a "peace at any price" kind of person, you are going to be a poor manager.

Then thirdly, the *authority of your personality.* The easier it is for the other fellow to talk to you, to listen to you or to work with you, the easier he will find it to respond to your wishes. On the one hand, authoritatively fill your position; on the other hand, be as human as you can possibly be. Position and personality are the two sides of the same coin.

Fourthly, the *authority of character.* This component is your credit rating with other people — that is, your reliability, honesty, loyalty, sincerity, and your personal morals and ethics. In the Philippines somebody said to me, "Mr. So and So? Oh, he is one of the outstanding preachers in the Republic of the Philippines, but I would not work with that man for anything. You cannot trust him. He will tell you one thing and tell somebody else on the staff just the opposite." No character, no integrity, no reliability, no trustworthiness! We manage by the authority of our character.

CHAPTER 7
UNDERSTAND
YOUR GROUP
The Two Basic Groups

THE TWO BASIC GROUPS

"In some of our minds, the Church exists in order to perpetuate its existence. The Church should exist in order to accomplish the goals its Lord has put before it."

The next subject is an analysis of the two basic groups or mentalities that prevail in the two extremes of group situations.

The Centric Group

The first type of group is the *centric group.* The centric group is an association of people — religious, educational, social, or industrial, in which the general level of personal concern is greater than the general level of group concern. The result is an introspection, a turning in upon the group itself.

With the centric group there is an incompatibility of objectives. Where there is an ingrown aspect, the people involved tend to give primacy to their own objectives rather than to the objectives of the group. Not only that, there is resistance to authority in the centric group. The centric group is generally control-oriented. Everyone is demanding to be heard. The centric group gives primary consideration to this question — "Are we structured so that everyone can have his say?"

I am not advocating any form of government. Every form of government can degenerate into a centric group and any form of government can be a goal-oriented group. There is a resistance to authority in the centric group. While this group is always centered in itself, it is never looking critically with regard to performance but always looking critically with regard to control. "Are we giving every man a right to say all that he feels?"

A mission organization that is centric in its association and functions from a group point of view is generally made up of mature people. Alone they are spiritually responsible, imaginative, poised and disciplined. But in a group situation all of these aspects of the centric group come to the fore. Why? I do not understand it, but I know that there is something about an association of people on certain topics that tends toward the centric aspect. Generally it is government, and it revolves around a question of decision-making or authority.

The Radic Group

There is another type of group — *the radic group.* This is the group in which the level of group concern is greater than the general level of personal concern.

Now, in discussing the centric and radic groups, do not assume that one is secular and the other is sacred. That is not necessarily true. Some of the most radic groups I know are utterly secular. For example, the U.S. Peace Corps. A lot of the humanitarian enterprises of the world are radic. The point is that this group tends to radiate out rather than turn in. In this group you have goal-orientation and perceptive team work. This is the type of group that Jesus Christ designed in both the apostolate and in the Church in its growth and development.

The Church was always to be a radic group, and it is a sign of our degeneracy when we become centric. In some of our minds, the Church exists in order to perpetuate its existence. The Church should exist in order to accomplish the goals its Lord has put before it. Quite a difference! Do we exist to perpetuate our existence? That is centric. Do we exist to accomplish our Lord's goal? That is radic. Generally, a group starts out radic and degenerates to centric. The extent to which we have become centric is the extent to which we have passed down the line through a work-orientation or a task-orientation to the bitter dregs of a control-orientation.

Management is not teaching somebody else something. Management is assimilating knowledge and beginning to demonstrate it and infecting people with it. This must be our strategy — not, "What can I teach this person in order to set him right?" but, "What can I learn to demonstrate in my managerial post that will become central in its growth?" Centric groups do not grow appreciably. Centric groups tend to stagnate, if not in the assimilation of new personnel, at least in the dynamics of their activity. Particularly this is true in religion because in religious types of work, we must attract people. Centric groups simply stop being attractive.

The chief danger for the radic group is in becoming so fragmented in its purposes that different groups and different individuals have different purposes and they begin to compete. This will always lead back into a centric orientation. It is not that any group is solidly radic. One aspect or the other tends to dominate.

Does the goal still grip us? Is it still worthy of our commitment? The danger here is to have one thing in writing and another thing in practice — a Jekyll and Hyde management practice.

It is much easier to train a group to function in accordance with a predescribed plan of conformity than it is to train a group to achieve a goal. I may say to my boy, "Now do this. No, you may not do that. Yes, do that. That's fine." Giving instructions is easier than saying, "Now, look, young man, you are to conduct yourself in an honorable, upright way so that at the end of your life you will be able to say, 'I have lived honorably and decently.'"

The Importance of the Goal

What holds the radic group together? It is the goal. The more we are obsessed with the goal, the more we are willing to tolerate individual differences within the organization. The less we are obsessed with the goal, the more we need to have personality conformity within the organization. Somebody comes to you and he does not say things just the way you would say them. If we are goal-orientated we say, "This man has something to contribute and we will endure much from him because he is going to help us reach our goal." The breadth of tolerance in the radic group is much greater than the breadth of tolerance in the centric group. A strong goal-oriented mission will tend to reproduce a strong goal-oriented church and a strong goal-oriented young people's movement within that church. The same principle applies. You have to start where you are, with the group you associate with. You cannot walk into another group, to which you are not responsible for leadership and direction, and say, "Here's how this ought to be done."

Single-Man Rule and Team Rule

There is another important phase of organization to cover: the two basic types of organizational structure. These are single-man rule and team rule.

Religious organizations come into existence and function best initially as a single-man rule. This is generally true but not always the case. The man with the burden gets the job. The man with the vision makes a decision. He is the person who has attracted men around him. He initiates a one-man rule. A dictatorship, whether it is in a religious environment or in a political situation, is always the most efficient form of government. If you have a benevolent dictator, you are in business. The problem is that dictators tend to become self-centered — even in religious situations. The issue here is DECISION-MAKING. Who decides what this person is going to do? How much money is he going to spend? Where is he going to work? Which house is he going to live in?

The alternative to this man making all the decisions is team work, multiple-man rule. I do not mean that the alternative to one man making all the decisions is everybody making the decisions. That is compounding the red tape which must be gone through in order to arrive at a decision. But the other alternative to one man deciding everything is to let everybody make what decisions they can in keeping with the information they have at hand and the competency they possess. *In other words, decisions should always be pushed down the organizational chart.* If you must err, err in asking a man to make too many decisions rather than in not asking him to make enough decisions.

Decisions should be made on the lowest possible level. Decisions should always be made as near as possible to where the work is actually performed. Unless a one-man ruler is tremendously goal-oriented, he will make as many decisions as he possibly can. Even a pastor, unless he is goal-oriented, will grasp for as much decision-making as he possibly can get. Why? To protect himself, and to be more comfortable. The only alternative I know of to insure that this man will constantly push decisions down is goal-orientation. Otherwise, our very nature will cause us to accumulate decisions at the top. This retards the progress of the whole group by forcing everything to be channeled through one man. But what does this do to the goal? We achieve goals best when people are allowed to make as many decisions as possible which affect their work. Let your aim be to push decision-making down the structure.

If the group is not committed to the goal, you might as well fall back and re-group. This assumes that a leader is constantly going to be training his people how to make decisions.

One of the men who reports to me came in some time ago. He had a thorny situation and he said, "What shall I do?"
"Let's discuss the facts," I said.

He laid the whole thing out before me, and I made some observations and asked some questions. We talked for some time about the problem.
"All right," he said, "What do you want me to do?"
I said, "This is your decision. I want you to make the decision. What do *you* want to do about it?"

It was important enough that I felt I had to know what the decision was, but he made the decision. I did not precisely agree. There were a couple of things I thought should be different, but they were not big enough for me to say, "Change that." I let him make his decision. That man grew a foot taller. If I had thought his decision was radically wrong, I would have explained why and I would have asked him to reconsider it.

Any man who cannot train decision-making capacities in the men under him is not worthy of being in a managerial position! The man at the top must make decisions that are major, that affect the overall situation or interpretation of policy.

There was a general in World War II whose fellow commanding officers got together and said, "We think such and such an attack ought to be made." The general said, "No, it won't work. We will lose too many men. Here is why it will not work." They considered. They over-rode this man who had to command his own men. They said, "Our decision is, we attack this way." He said, "I disagree. These are my men, and we are going to lose." They replied, "This is what we're going to do anyway." He yielded and sure enough his predictions were right. He lost many men. His own subordinate officers came back and asked, "Why?" The general said, "Our decision was..." and he never once indicated that he had differed.

It is the absence of this kind of courage that causes friction in churches and mission groups. If you do not agree with what "they" say, are you going to go along? What alternative do you have? The alternative is to split the group and to set "your" people at variance with one another. You can create your own little domain if that is what you want, or you can get out. The stronger the goal-orientation, the stronger a leader will strive for cohesiveness. The less the goal-orientation, the more content a leader will be to develop his own little domain. How do you build manliness or courage? I really do not know except to develop it yourself and hope it will rub off on the person that is watching you. I think the more important the goal is to us, the more courageous we are to try to achieve it.

Let us make a distinction. If a man comes to me and says, "I want to talk to you personally and confidentially," that is no problem. But if he wants to talk to me personally and confidentially about the work, there can be no such thing as a personal and confidential conversation because it involves others. If it is a problem in his own life and his own family situation, that is personal. But if it involves a group goal, it is no longer personal. Tell people everything you can and you will seldom be called upon to tell them things you should not. If they know you are open and not secretive, they will not suspect you of withholding information.

CHAPTER 8
SHARE THE TASK
Delegation and Job Descriptions

SHARE THE TASK

"'A job description helps us know what our tasks are and why we are in the organization. A job description helps our boss to know what we are doing. It helps us to know what he expects of us, and it lets people around us know what we are doing. Likewise we know why their jobs exist.''

What is Delegation?

Delegation is one of the activities under the heading of Management Organizing. There are three components. But first, a definition. What do we mean by delegation? In a recent book, *The Effective Executive,* Peter Drucker has three diagnostic questions for the effective managing of *time.* When Drucker first got into management consulting, he realized that he had to have some way of quickly sizing up an organization, what it was doing, what it was like, and what its needs were. He came up with three diagnostic questions:

1. What am I doing that really does not need to be done at all by me or anyone else?
2. Which of the activities on my time log could be handled by someone else as well if not better?
3. What do I do that wastes the time of other people?

Amplifying on these three points, Drucker went on to say that he discovered that a well-managed plant, office, business, organization is always dull-DULL! *The recurrent crisis is by far the most common symptom of poor management.* I think he is right.

Now, what is delegation? Many attempts have been made to define delegation. One, for example, says, "Delegation is giving others the right to make your decisions." Another says, "Delegation is to give authority to accompany responsibility." "Delegation is having other people do part of your work" is still another. I think all of these are inadequate. I would like us to agree on L.A. Allen's definition that, "Delegation is entrusting responsibility and authority and establishing lines of accountability."

Delegation is learning how to identify the work that we are doing and devising methods of passing these pieces of work on to other people, but maintaining a management check on these activities.

In Japan one of our Japanese pastors came to me and said, "Mr. Hendrix, I would like to ask you a question." I braced myself. He said, "There is an old Japanese proverb and I want to ask you if you think this proverb is true and accurate. It goes this way: 'A wise prince or lord knows even how many ashes are in the stove in the kitchen.' Is this a good proverb?" I tried to figure out what he was getting at and answered, "No, that is not a good proverb. A wise prince or lord does not necessarily know how many ashes there are in the stove, but he knows he has someone who does know how many ashes are in the kitchen stove." The pastor smiled. I am afraid I gave him some ammunition against some of my colleagues. Not that he needed it — I think he had enough of his own.

The Need for Delegation. Why should we consider delegation? Here are some reasons for delegating:

1. *You are not doing the big jobs that need to be done.* That is your job as the top executive. Someone says, "Communications have broken down in our church." Someone else says, "I don't know what my job is." That is your job, to help them find out what their job is. Demoralization has set in. Your job is to work on that. If you are not doing these big jobs that need to be done, you should consider delegation.

2. *You are missing deadlines*. One day I sat down with Clarence Jones before I made my first trip overseas and I said, "Clarence, you are a veteran, traveling everywhere, teaching people and lecturing on various subjects. Give me some guidelines. Tell me what to do and what not to do as I make this trip." He said, "Well, it is important to work on other people's time clock. Do not take your own American time clock."

I have tried to do this and I know that deadlines are not as important in some cultures as they are in others. I know, for example, that in Japan the more important a letter is, the more time you give to contemplation before you answer it. An immediate response, instead of being the epitome of efficiency, is the representation of laxity and unconcern. I know that about Japan. However, where deadlines are set, you should meet them. Sometimes you are caught in cross-cultural situations where to miss deadlines is to create demoralization in a staff. If you are missing deadlines, if you are backlogged so that you cannot get things done when they are supposed to be done, you need to consider delegation.

3. *You now spend time on trivial tasks that others could do.* Here, we often face a problem of false modesty when we say, "Well, I'm not too good. I can't do that." We come to our service for Jesus Christ, recognizing that there are some things which we will do that no one else is eager to do. But we must not let trivial tasks force us into a corner, particularly when all they do is feed our own ego and our estimation of how humble we are.

4. *You have men who, if trained, could handle the job better than you*. One of our biggest problems in Christian work is our failure to properly appraise the potentialities of the people with whom we work. Having done so honestly we serve both the individual and the organization well when we pass on challenging and rewarding tasks to others.

5. *You have an imbalance in the work load of your men.* Some of our men are underworked and others are overworked. You must help the overloaded to learn to delegate for themselves. One of the hardest things in the world is to teach a person to look always at his work with the view, "Who can I get to do this so that I can give myself to a more important task?" We allow things that we do ourselves to become boss-imposed and

system-imposed activities, instead of pushing them out and seeing that other people get them done. But often it is easier, and more comfortable when we do it ourselves. That is reverting to operating instead of managing.

6. *You have men who need new worlds to conquer.* They need new spheres of responsibility. People need to grow. A frequent reason given for leaving an organization is the feeling that there is no where left to go.

The Ethics of Delegation. For a long time I ran into all kinds of resistance when I talked about delegation, and I could not understand it. Why do Christian workers fight the concept of delegation? Finally, one man said to me, "How can I give someone else the right, authority and assignment to do what God has called *me* to do?" I realized this was an ethical problem. This problem is very real and I do not minimize it. If God has called me to do something, then I cannot easily or lightly turn away from that and let somebody else take it up. But I think this ethical problem is answered completely by going back again to the three ingredients of delegation, principally emphasizing accountability. Although I have delegated a piece of work, I retain ultimately the responsibility for its performance. Many times people have demonstrated to me their frustration because they gave somebody something to do and then, at the last minute, they discovered that it had not been done. Who is responsible? In the final analysis, those who delegated are responsible. I think this answers, then, the ethical question that comes with regard to delegation. If I give somebody else a job to do and have an understanding that they are going to do it, I cannot just turn my back and walk away from it. I am still responsible, and if it does not get done I have to answer for it. Mr. Harry Truman in his Presidential office used to have a sign worth remembering, "The buck stops here." Every manager ought to have that mentality. I am responsible and from this office there is no "passing the buck!" If the person did not do it, it is my fault.

Henry Brandt says, "People do what we *inspect* not what we *expect.*" And it simply means that you have to solemnly and relentlessly inspect and establish lines for accountability. You have to accept that the best man you have may not be able to follow through on a given assignment unless you continually supervise and check back and give concern, help and direction. To me this answers the ethical question.

We are always in a state of conflict concerning what we would like to do and what we are gifted to do. People who have been in the ministry fifty years are still struggling with it. I do not have an easy answer, but I have developed some answers that satisfy me. I have decided never to desire to do anything that requires gifts my brethren do not recognize in me. I am not an individualist. I am a member of the body, a part of the organization. I will continually accept that I tend to have exaggerated notions of my abilities.

Reasons for Resistance to Delegation

There are some barriers to delegation. Why is it that delegation is so difficult? Here are some reasons for resistance to delegation:

1. There is a reluctance to admit limitation. We don't like to admit that we can't easily do something. There are always people who are willing to take real responsibility for some segment of the work if the other person is willing to let go. The biggest problem is getting the person at the top to let go.

2. Tradition, desire for prestige, desire to retain control.

3. Lack of confidence in your men. The more insecure we are, the more we tend to look with disdain upon the capacity of the people around us because, we think, that makes us look better or bigger. Why is this? I am not sure that I know the reason, but we ought to be *the* people of all people who are poised and confident. Is it that we are possessive of our positions and defensive of our organizations and have only a minimum of goal commitment?

4. You doubt your ability to train someone else to do it your way. Many times our appraisal is on the basis of "how" something is done, not "whether" it is done.

5. Ignorance. Some of us have never seen it done properly.

Let us summarize. We have said that all of the reasons for a man resisting delegation are within him, not outside him. All the reasons for resisting delegation are emotional. It is something within him that blocks him, not something from without.

The subject of *Job Description* relates dynamically and vitally to the entire plan, lead, organize, control concept. Let us look again at the outline and relate the subject of Job Descriptions to it. There are two places where job descriptions might be considered. I believe Louis Allen inserts job descriptions into the subject of establishing objectives. Job descriptions can be there or under the subject of delegating. I feel it belongs under objectives because normally delegation has to do with situations that are not covered in a formal job description. Here we take objectives as referring not only to corporate and departmental, but also to individual responsibilities.

The Need for Job Descriptions

The extent to which you grasp this may determine largely the relevance of this book to your future. I hope you will see how this subject can relate to your own situation. It is my absolute conviction that all of us in Christian work should have job descriptions and those job descriptions should be living, dynamic tools like the organizational structure. A job description, if it has not been reviewed with the people concerned, the boss and the subordinate, at least once a year, up-dated, retyped and re-issued, it is antiquated. It may be doing more harm than good.

Job descriptions are very important. A job description helps us know what our tasks are and why we are in the organization. A job description helps our boss to know what we are doing. It helps us to know what he expects of us, and it lets people around us know what we are doing. Likewise we know why their jobs exist. Very few people in industry have job descriptions. Many businesses do not have job descriptions. If they do, often they are unrelated, irrelevant, out of date and quite a caricature — not really representative of what the person is doing — in which case it is tragic.

The more technical and specific and routine the function, the easier it is to write the job description but the less the description is needed. The more innovative, creative, and imaginative the job, the greater the need for the job description but the more difficult to write. For example, a person doing linguistic work is assigned to a tribe to reduce a language to writing. It is easy, relatively speaking, to write that man's job description. But a job assigned to a church planter is very difficult to write, yet this man needs a description even more than the linguist. The more technical the work, the easier it is to write the job description. Take a situation in the Missionary Aviation Fellowship (MAF). It will be a great deal easier to write the job description of a man whose job it is to repair engines than it is to write the job description for the man who is the Field Director. The more managerial the job, the more difficult to write the description. But the more managerial the function, the more important it is to write the job description.

Job descriptions show us what we are supposed to do and show our boss what we are doing. Even if you are in a voluntary situation where you are not paid at all, job descriptions are still important. Some of the most effective churches I know in America have job descriptions for their deacons and their Sunday School superintendents and their Sunday School teachers. And you might think that people stand off and say, "Oh, I don't want a job description. I'm just serving the Lord." But these people say, "I'm glad to know what is expected of me." It puts teeth into our organizational structure, and it gives clarity to relationships. More than any other single device, job descriptions give us a goal-orientation.

The best job descriptions are specific, definite, and measurable. They have teeth; they are binding; they are clear.

In a seminar some time ago I gave a lecture on job descriptions and then assigned the people to write down their own job descriptions. Here is the job description that I received. It followed my suggested format — the job summary, the job duties, the organizational relationships, the qualifications and the development. What do you think of this? "JOB SUMMARY — To live in a certain village in such a spiritual, Christ-honoring way as to turn residents of this village from darkness to light. JOB DUTIES — 1) To maintain a constant fellowship with God, so as to live a sinless, perfect example in dependence upon the Holy Spirit. 2) Be ready at all times to give a reason for the hope that is in you. 3) Give unselfishly of your time and talents to any worthy cause within the village which might result in winning some. 4) Write a report at least once a month. ORGANIZATIONAL RELATIONSHIPS — Responsible to God alone — He who will judge the quick and the dead. Responsible for — those in the village whom God has predestinated to enter into His glorious fellowship. QUALIFICATIONS — should be a spiritually-minded person of highest integrity; if possible, should have completed Bible School. TRAINING AND DEVELOPMENT — should be skilled in using the Word of God for the winning of precious souls.''

In the light of what I said the job description ought to be, this job description is ambiguous and has no measurement, but it sounds so spiritual! Do you know what good this will do? It will just inflate the man's already overinflated spiritual ego.

The kind of job description format you use is unimportant. Go to the library and check a hundred books on management in which the subject of job descriptions is dealt with and you will find a hundred suggestions or formats. For example, there was an article recently on how to write a job description for a pastor. The format was altogether different than what I would suggest, but in the end it accomplished the same thing. Generally, they all come out at the same place, though the building of them is entirely different.

Writing the Job Description

First, at the beginning of your job description you need a Job Title. The Job Title should be as descriptive as possible of the work that is performed. Where you are involved with precedent and tradition and cannot make changes, use whatever terms the situation dictates. The title should describe as nearly as possible the work that is being filled or accomplished by this position. Then, you need the name of the individual involved. There are only two places where the specific individual himself is brought into play — at the top of the sheet and in the last point, *TRAINING AND DEVELOPMENT.*

The other sections of this job description could apply to any individual. Next, write the date. This is important because once twelve months have elapsed, it is out of date! There are very few job descriptions that can go on for more than a year without alterations, because the environment changes, the capacities of the individual change and the needs of the office change. The person managing has to keep this constantly in review. In more intricate, complex situations you may want to indicate the department or the division. For example, a person may be in the Evangelism Department, the Church-Planting Department, or the Radio Department of a mission, or he may be in the Laboratory Department of a hospital. This simply further breaks down and pinpoints where this man fits in the organization. Adapt these any way you see fit to meet the demands of your organization.

The job description consists of five parts:

1. *THE JOB SUMMARY.* This is the most difficult to write. The Job Summary reflects the position of the organizational chart. The Job Summary is built into that total pyramid (see page 58). There should be a short-range and a long-range pyramid. The Job Summary places a person into the pyramid where he belongs, and is aimed at accomplishing the goal of the total organization. The Job Summary puts in words the end result this position exists to accomplish. Particularly when you ask someone for whom you are responsible to begin working on their own job description, you are going to find that sometimes they do not know why they are there. This has to do with purpose, with objectives, with goals, with targets. Not only this but you are going to discover that you have positions for which there is no valid reason for continued existence. If you take this matter seriously, you will find that there are people on the payroll involved in the activities who have no definitive, specific purpose for their operation. The Job Summary, the end result the job exists to accomplish, is the most difficult part to write in all of the job description. It must be measurable, definitive and specific.

2. *THE JOB DUTIES.* These are the activities necessary for the accomplishment of the above-mentioned end result. This is the easiest to write, particularly if you just write down what the person is presently doing. If that is all you do, you have not

written a job description. You have only given the man a piece of paper to justify the continuation of his activities, and that may be bad. Do not come to *DUTIES* until you have settled the end result.

Once this is settled, you will want to list the activities that are necessary for the accomplishment of the above-mentioned end result. Here you begin to draw some very distinct lines between the various positions that exist in your organization, and begin to eliminate overlap. This can help the function of an organization where a man, while he retains an extremely sensitive team-consciousness and concept, recognizes "I'm praying for this man over here who is doing so and so, but that is his job and this is mine." He is concerned and is involved. He is available to help if he is needed, but that is not his job and he does not interfere. Even though he is the manager he is not going to make another man's decision. He has his own work to do.

3. *ORGANIZATIONAL RELATIONSHIPS.* Here we are back to the organizational chart. Organizational relationships extend in four directions: up, down, and sideways in both directions. This should show a man exactly what his relationship is to his superior, exactly what his relationship is to his subordinate and what his relationship is to the people on either side of him. This works in a church where a Sunday School department leader realizes "I take my orders with respect to the operation of this Sunday School from Mr. So and So. I am responsible to oversee these people. I know there is another department functioning over here and this man has the same kind of authority and responsibility that I have." You do not have to pay a man a salary in order to do this. It works beautifully in a voluntary situation like a Sunday School or in a more complex situation like General Motors. The two key words are TO and FOR. *Responsible to* — that shows superiors; *responsible for* — that designates subordinates.

It is important to note the difference between "staff" and "line" relationships. A staff relationship means service, information, consultation and advice. This person or committee has no authority. He does not issue any orders. In the chart, the broken line indicates a "staff" relationship over against a "line relationship." In other words, this man or group serves in an advisory capacity rather than in an authoritative and decision-making role.

4. *QUALIFICATIONS*. These are for the performance of the work. This is what the person should *ideally* be and know in order to most effectively accomplish the Job Summary. If you omit the individual's name then you can write job descriptions for functions you eventually want accomplished in your organization for which you neither have men nor money now. This helps tremendously. It is not a matter of who is available; it is a matter of "here is what we want done. Where is the person that can best do it?" That makes a difference in filling positions in your church. Here is what we are trying to accomplish by this church and what needs to be done in this position. Here are the qualifications. Where is the man? You set your standard high, but keep it realistic.

At this point you specify the job description under the heading of Training and Development.

5. *TRAINING AND DEVELOPMENT.* In other words, this man does not ever measure up fully to these qualifications. He needs self-development to better qualify. We are speaking here about skills and abilities — about learning in order to do better the job he has been called by God to do. That is self-development. If the key to training and development is that it must be specific, then training and development must project itself for no more than twelve months.

This man does not quite measure up. No man does. If he does, revise your qualifications and get them up higher. What training and development can we give to this man in order to better qualify him? You do not unilaterally determine this and hand it to him on a slip of paper as you go past him one morning. This is a mutually agreed thing. He will be harder on himself than you would be if you let him be. Do not think of training and development as just going to school. You can learn without going to a university. There are other places to develop your skills. For example, one of our men needed development in a certain area. We inquired around and did some research and found, as far as we were able to determine, the one man in America that knew more about this subject than any other man. We wrote to him and said, "If we send our man out, can he sit at your elbow for a couple of weeks and just watch what you do?'' That is training and develoment.

Training and development says, ''Mr. A. is going to California. He is going to be an understudy with Mr. B. from October 1 to October 15. It will cost us 'X' number of dollars.'' That is training and development. It may include formal situations. Training and development does not necessarily mean going back to seminary. That is not the kind of training and development most of us need. Sometimes we may need a Dale Carnegie course, or a rapid-reading course, or a course in public relations, or a course in some skill that relates to the type of work that we are doing. This training and development is specific. It is dated. It is to compensate for the man's inadequacies as they are spelled out in this list of qualifications. I know this is work, but it will transform any operation you are in — if you will do it.

CHAPTER 9
ENCOURAGE
THE TROOPS
Management Leading Principles

MANAGEMENT LEADING PRINCIPLES

"There is a vast difference between problem-identification and problem-solving. Problem-solving, comparatively speaking is easy. Problem-identification is extremely difficult."

Under the subject of management-leading comes decision-making and communicating. Leading is the work in which we engage to inspire and, where necessary, impel people to take action. But in order to lead effectively, we must know how to make decisions and how to effectively communicate.

Let us first consider the subject of decision-making.

A. *DECISION-MAKING*

Someone described a manager as a man who makes decisions. Sometimes he makes the right ones, sometimes he makes the wrong ones, but he always makes them. We must not insist upon infallibility in decision-making for people who work with us, nor in ourselves.

If you are in a place of leadership you have to make decisions. Hesitancy on your part in deciding will breed demoralization and frustration among your followers. The longer it takes a man to get a decision from you, the more encumbered he is and the more you are saying to that man, "Your time and activities are of minimal importance."

Why do we have such difficulties in making decisions? One major reason is the control-orientation of our organization. We would prefer to have everyone involved in the decision than to have the decision made quickly, effectively and thereby accomplish our goal. To make decisions involves risk. Many people hedge on decision-making and would prefer to do anything rather than to decide.

Decision Making Principles

There are three principles which apply to decision-making.

First, a logical decision can be reached only if the problem is first defined. There is a vast difference between problem-identification and problem-solving. Problem-solving, comparatively speaking, is easy. Problem-identification is extremely difficult. Most of us do not take time to identify problems. We plunge in to solve them. Problems, because they are related to human beings, are often covered with a facade -- one of the chief characteristics of the human being. When you sit down with an individual and say, ''How are you?'' he will seldom tell you right off how he really is. A person comes to you for counselling. ''Tell me what your problem is'' you begin. He will seldom say at first what his real problem is. Because problems are so intimately entwined with human emotions, we have difficulty facing the heart of the problem. We must be careful to avoid dealing with just the symptoms, while avoiding the real problem. We must persevere to adequately define the problem.

Second, the principle of adequate evidence teaches us that a logical decision must be valid in terms of the evidence upon which it is based. Our problem in God's work is our utter subjectivity. Our subjectivity builds a high protective wall around us so that everything about us is immune to the criticism of our fellow men because we have prayed about it, or the Lord has led us. I am not speaking lightly about prayer or of divine guidance. But if a person is not very careful, this subjectivity can become a protective wall around an individual to keep him from the truth.

Third, the principle of identify or scope. This principle teaches us that facts may appear to differ, depending upon the point of view and the point in time from which they are observed. In other words, the decisions we make are valid or invalid depending upon how and when we look at them. This is why some decisions made today look so stupid tomorrow.

The Logical Thinking Process

Next, let us consider the logical thinking process. It consists of a series of questions. I do not expect that you are going to take these questions and apply them to every decision. But if you can apply them to major decisions, they will help you immeasurably. They will form a pattern in your subconscious mind in adapting to various types of problem situations. The questions in the logical thinking process, in order, are as follows:

1. *What is The Apparent Problem?* What do you think is the problem? It may not be the real problem.

2. *What Are The Facts?* Because some of us are exclusively theologically-oriented and think we have a pipeline to omniscience, we cannot afford to be bothered with the assimilation of facts. After all, we have revelation! Somebody once asked, ''Are you gathering facts or merely rearranging your prejudices?'' Here you need to get the situation factor, the people factor, the place factor, the time factor, the causative factor, and then assimilate all the facts you can.

3. *What Is The Real Problem?* Do not ask this question until you have adequately dealt with the two previous ones! Remember the facade!

4. *What Are The Possible Solutions?* Generally, the possible solutions that emerge spontaneously to your mind will be extremes. That is the way we solve problems instinctively. We just get hold of the pendulum and swing as hard as we can from one extreme to the other. These extreme solutions may need to be considered, but do not settle for two alternative and diametrically opposed solutions. *There is always a third solution.* It will seldom manifest itself easily, but do not stop until you find a third solution to the problem. When you find the third, you will often find that it will open up a whole new vista with a fourth, fifth and sixth possible solution.

5. *What Course Of Action Shall We Follow?* This involves implementation of the course chosen. Risk becomes a prime factor. If you have a "safety first" mentality all of your analysis and fact assimilation will come to nothing here.

Four questions which outline the total analysis required by any decision large or small:

1. Do I really understand the problem?
2. What am I trying to get done?
3. Is this the way to do it?
4. What will go wrong when I put this decision into action?

You are not going to solve one problem without creating others. However, you hope to create lesser problems. Nevertheless, in most problem solving there are some negative consequences. Anticipate them. What is going to go wrong when I put this decision into effect?

B. *COMMUNICATIONS*

What is communication? I want to give you a definition from the Word of God. In this passage there is one word which, more than any other word, tells us what communication is. I Cor. 14:7-9 "And even things without life giving sound, whether pipe or harp, except they give a distinction in the sounds, how shall it be known what is piped or harped? For if the trumpet give an uncertain sound, who shall prepare himself for battle? So, likewise, except ye utter by the tongue words easy to be understood, how shall it be known what is spoken? For ye shall speak into the air." (A.V.) It is the word, "understood" that is so important. Communication is the work we do to secure *understanding* between ourselves and another human being.

David Sarnoff of RCA said, "The power to communicate is the power to lead." I do not think anyone who has been involved in a managerial position will doubt this assertion.

Principles of Communication

In management-leading there are three principles which apply to communication:

1. *The principle of line loss.* The effectiveness of communication tends to vary inversely with its extension. Suppose I took

fifteen men, lined them up around the room, and then read in the ear of one man a headline from the morning paper. By the time that headline was transmitted orally from man to man around the room, there would be little or no resemblance with what came from man fifteen as compared with what went into man one! The effectiveness of communication tends to vary inversely with its extension. The more levels it has to go through, the more minds and tongues that filter it, the more distorted it becomes. There is no sense in getting angry about this and there is no sense in blaming people when something is repeated back to you, fifth or sixth hand, and you are quoted incorrectly.

2. *The principal of emotional appeal.* Appeals to emotions are communicated more readily than appeals to reason. If you preachers could get hold of this it could revolutionize your preaching. We are so logical. We follow such strict forms of apologetics and we have everything unanswerably set forth. The only problem is that no one hears it. It does not grip anyone. Study the great teachers and preachers of history and you will find that they have always found emotional pegs upon which to hang their thoughts.

3. *The principle of application.* The more a specific communication is used and applied, the better it will be understood and remembered. Some of us do a lot of talking but not much teaching — a lot of preaching but not much communicating. Why? Because maybe we only say it once or twice, or a dozen times, and that is not enough. Sometimes a thing has to be said over and over and over again.

The big problem in communication Is words -- because words tend to obscure meaning and not clarify. According to the Oxford English Dictionary, the five hundred most-used words in the English language have an average of twenty-three meanings each. The word "round" has seventy distinctly different meanings. This is not the only problem we face.

The problem that we are confronted with is that we have a man with an idea. He wants to communicate that idea to another person. How is he going to transmit an idea from his brain to the other person's brain? It can be a theological idea, a mechanical idea, a philosophical idea, etc. Obviously, his first recourse is going to be words. They may be written or spoken, softly or loudly. Words are the main instrument at his disposal to communicate or transmit this idea from his mind to another human being's mind. The words may have one meaning in the mind of the speaker, but a completely different meaning in the mind of the hearer.

Dr. Howard Hendricks of Dallas Theological Seminary describes the difficulty in conveying not just a concept but a "concept feeling." His point is that we do not convey concepts only. That is impossible. We convey "concept feelings." The two are inseparable. It is not just a cold idea. It is an idea that is coupled with feeling. Sometimes it is an intense feeling; sometimes not so intense; sometimes a negative feeling. Sometimes a feeling of hate or love. Still there is a feeling to some degree connected with every concept, and these feelings color our hearing!

Four Stages of Communication

Why do we get into such trouble when it comes to communication? Because there are four stages in the process of communication and often we go astray at *each* stage.

1. *We begin with the all-important process of asking.* We do not adequately communicate with another until we have asked questions. I must know the person's mind in some degree before I can communicate with him. The complexity and the intricacies of the message determine how much I must know about that person's mind. For example, if I want to say, "Shut the door," I do not have to know a great deal about the person or his thinking processes in order to communicate that concept. But let us say I want to communicate a theological or philosophical idea to this fellow. Where he was born, how he was brought up, what his family situation was like, where he went to school, what books he has read in the last five years -- a thousand things can enter in here.

How do I discover what another human being is like? By looking at the color of his skin? By looking at the color of his eyes? By looking at whether he is fat or skinny? NO! These are externals. They have nothing to do with what is inside the man. There is one way you get to the man on the inside and that is to ask questions. Some of us do not communicate simply because we either do not have the time to ask questions or we do not know how to ask questions.

There are three basic types of questions:

First, there is the *informational* type question. These have to do with statistics and facts. Questions like: How many? Who? How much? Where? When? Informational questions are inoffensive questions. You can always say to a person, "Where do you work?" "How many people are involved?" without getting a negative reaction.

Second, there is the *ideational* type question. This is where you ask the person what he thinks or what he suggests or what he feels. Like informational questions, ideational questions are also safe. You will not create trouble or give offense when you are asking a subordinate ideational question.

The third type of question is different. This is the *evaluation* question and is always dangerous. This is where you ask a man to evaluate his work, his ideas, his concepts, or anything with which he is associated or involved. These kinds of questions are strategic and tend to become tremendously subjective. If you ask evaluative questions of an individual before you have asked ideational or informational questions you may alienate him. We are what we are and it is a proven fact that we are more willing to give evaluative information after we have had an opportunity to express our ideas and to give information, particularly information which we feel the other person may not have about us or our work. We need to ask questions that fit the need.

Questions to Ask

In all of this I am suggesting that you ask *"open questions"* not *"closed questions."* Open questions invite the other person to express freely what he feels. They never make him feel that he is boxed in. Here is an example of an open question: "Tell me, Joe, how does this problem look to you?" The person can go on from that to express what he really feels. A closed question is a kind of question that forces the other person to a point of view other than his own. It is a kind of question that makes him feel like he has to conform to what we already think. Here is an example of a closed question: "Now, Joe, if you were convinced that taking this action is morally wrong, you wouldn't be for it would you?'' What can he say? You have closed him out.

Ask leading questions, not loaded ones! Leading questions give direction to the reply but they are not restrictive to any one way. Here is an example of a leading question: ''How did you go about working out your solution to the problem, Joe?'' A loaded question puts the respondent in a difficult position -- whatever his answer may be. An example of a loaded question is: ''What made you think that your solution to the problem was the right one?'' You have made this fellow defensive. Defensiveness is one of the most detrimental and continuously recurring attitudes in Christian work. Not hatred. Not animosity. Not bitterness. I see these things occasionally, but the most universal attitude I find in Christian work is defensiveness.

Ask cool questions and not heated ones. The cool question appeals to reason and involves the emotion as little as possible. A heated question, on the other hand, reflects the feeling of the questioner and incites the feelings of the respondent. Here is the cool question: ''Now what would you say the first step towards a solution should be, Joe?'' And the heated question: ''We've already been round and round on that one, so what do you think we should do?'' The person has to produce there or be embarrassed.

2. *The second step in the communication process is telling* -- articulating -- putting in words the message you have to get across. Unfortunately, we often plunge into telling before we have done any asking. How do we go about telling? I am going to digress considerably from purely managerial communication situations to talk about communications in general because most of you who read this book are preachers and teachers. How do we communicate our message from our minds to the minds of a group of people? Here are four steps to good telling:

Four Steps to Good Telling

The first step is -- Get an audience. Attract attention! Here is a brain that is in absolute neutral, an emotion that is disengaged, an anatomy in which no capacity for receiving communication is presently functioning. The person may be in church or in Sunday School or in a seminar, but there he sits -- in neutral! Getting an audience is not easy.

There was a farmer who sold a mule to a person down the road. He explained carefully to the purchaser,

"This mule is a good ole mule but you must be gentle with him, ever so gentle.

The next day about ten o'clock, the purchaser appeared at the door of the seller, most irate, demanding his money back. The seller said,

"What's wrong?"

"That mule is sitting in the middle of the barnyard and will not move. I have been ever so gentle all morning with him and there he sits."

"Oh," the seller said, "Let me help you."

So they went down to the purchaser's barnyard and there sat the mule. He looked around the barnyard. He got a big stick and walked over to the mule and hit him as hard as he could right on the head. The old mule staggered around and got up on his feet. The man said,

"But I thought you said you had to be gentle."

"You do, but first you have to get his attention!"

We often talk without getting anyone's attention.

Step two in good telling is, *Build a bridge.* Build a bridge from what you say to what he is interested in. I like young people. I would rather smell perfume than liniment! I like young people -- their imagination, their drive, their color, the sparkle in their eyes. Frankly, I do not think that all young people have deteriorated. But, the one complaint I hear most frequently from young people about preaching in America is, "Well, what's all that got to do with where I am? Why bring that up? We hear these learned dissertations on this subject and that, but they are wide of the mark. They make no point of contact with us." We cannot get through to them until we learn to build a bridge from where we are to where they are.

Number three, *Illustrate*! You may have heard Dr. Donald Grey Barnhouse preach. In my estimation, Dr. Barnhouse was one of the greatest illustrators ever and also one of the best communicators. I would recommend that you read his sermons and books. The man was masterful. Also study the illustrations of the New Testament. You will find that in most instances

Bible illustrations use things that people handle and with which they are thoroughly conversant and familiar.

Point number four in good telling is, *Ask for action*. We might say this about almost any communication. There is a sense in which the whole point of a communication is to ask for action.

Sue Nichols, in her book *Words on Target* says that there are three essential ingredients in communication. These are:

1. We must communicate *economically*. There must be economy in our communication. Economy in communication means communicating without any unnecessary words. Play back one of your sermons sometime. Listen to the superfluous words. What do they do? They obstruct communication.

2. We must communicate with words of *energy*, words of force. How long has it been since you added a new word to your vocabulary? This is one thing you can do. All of you probably have access to the *Reader's Digest*. Work those little vocabulary builders. Make it a point to learn at least one new word every week and make sure they are easy words. Make sure they are words that will carry an impact. Some of you may have heard Dr. R.G. Lee, one of the greatest preachers of our day, an orator *par excellence*. Somebody was complimenting Lee one day on a sermon.

They said, ''Dr. Lee, the thing that is so unforgettable is your choice of words.''

He said, ''Oh, don't talk to me about words. I struggle with words.''

We do not take very seriously our vocabulary. Work on it. Discover words of energy to convey to your men.

3. We must communicate by *subtlety*. Ms. Nichols's point is that we must be the readers' eyes and ears, but we dare not be his brain or his will.

Listening is the third stage in the process of communication. We have tried to learn how to do about everything but listen. Andrew Carnegie said, ''Any fool can speak with a glib tongue. Send me a man who listens.'' A lot of us do not communicate because we do not listen. How many times people have said about another person, "I cannot get his ear." This is a sad commentary. Learn how to listen.

4. In the process of communication the final stage is *understanding*. This means that two human beings understand each other. Notice that communication is not agreement, but it is understanding. There is a lot more misunderstanding than there is disagreement among God's people. It is a strategic fact that the greater the level of understanding between people the higher the level of tolerance of disagreement.

Formal vs. Informal Communication

Let me clarify the difference between *formal* and *informal* communication. By formal communication we mean those words or letters by which we endeavor to formulate or convey a concept from ourselves to another person.

But this is not the only way we communicate. We communicate not only by what we say but also by how we say it, by our posture, our facial expressions, by the way we dress. Everything about us communicates! When a person drums his fingers on the table or desk, what does this say? It says volumes. "I'm bored and you are not important, so hurry up." It makes a difference how we carry ourselves, whether our shoulders are back or slumped. Do we not communicate by a positive attitude as over against a negative attitude? Do we not communicate by a spring in our step rather than a slouch in our walk? Everything about us communicates. This is why we need to consider everything that we are in our communication, the way we dress, the way we live, the way we express ourselves. This is information communication.

What are the barriers to communication? Where do we get into trouble? What causes our problems? Undoubtedly the biggest problem is our mistaking the medium for the process. Let me illustrate. I was conducting some meetings in a church in Michigan. After one of the meetings, a group of us were standing around in the basement of the church having coffee. The pastor's wife entered the room and she was what one might call a "female dread-naught." She steamed up to where I was, her eyes flaming with indignation. I stood there wondering whether to speak or run. After some minutes, I said,

"Hello," but she just puffed and steamed. Finally I said, "Is something wrong?" Well, that was pushing her button.

She said, "Those crazy women!"

I said, "Which women?"

She replied, "Those dumb women in our church."

I said, "Tell me about them."

Well did she ever tell me! Her whole point was "I told these people! I TOLD THESE WOMEN!" And I could not say it to her, but I thought to myself, "Yes, she told them, but that is not important. The important thing is, *did they hear her*?" It is an amazing thing. I can stand, or you can stand, in the presence of another person and tell and tell and tell and still have them say, "Nobody ever told me." It happens every day of the week to every one of us. My seventeen year old son came out one day with something that he had discovered. I had been telling him the same thing for seventeen years. He never heard it, but he heard someone else say it and it registered. What was my reaction? "Well, that's great! A great discovery, Dave! I'm happy for you. Terrific!" I'm not going to tell him, "Why, I told you that!" What difference does it make? We have an exaggerated concept of the significance of what we have to say. The other fellow does not care what we have to say. When you mistake the medium for the process you have not communicated. You may have told until you were hoarse. Communication is not telling. Communication is asking, telling, listening, and then creating understanding. It is nothing less than that. Communication is not writing a memo, for that does not ensure understanding.

The other barrier to communication is the failure to consider emotional blocks in communication. The fact, whether we like it or not, is that we are dealing with emotional creatures. You have something to tell someone. He may be inwardly distraught about things that he cannot divulge to you or anyone else. He is not going to hear what you say because he is preoccupied with his own distraction. He may be ill. Maybe he is not in pain enough that it warrants going to bed, but when a man is in pain he is preoccupied with that pain and he does not hear everything that goes on around him. Maybe he is distressed about one of his children. Or maybe something, in all innocence, was said two hours earlier which hurt that man. You may preach that self and feelings should not be felt. There is an element of truth in this, but we must remember that we are human beings.

We are communicating with people who are human beings. The Lord Jesus understood people, their feelings, their needs and He was sympathetic with them. He knew how to say precisely the right word to an adulteress. He knew exactly how to tenderly deal with those obstinate, impenetrable minds of the disciples. Read, *The Training of the Twelve*, by A.B. Bruce. See the marvelous empathy the Lord Jesus had for those men in their obstinacy, in their darkness -- the amazing ability of projecting His personality into the disciples and so fully understanding them. The Lord had this empathy for all whom He met. When He raised Jairus' daughter from the dead, the first thing He said was, ''Give her something to eat.'' We would have been more interested in getting a tract written, but not the Lord Jesus. ''Give her something to eat.''

CHAPTER 10
EVALUATE
THE RESULTS
Management Controlling
Principles and Styles

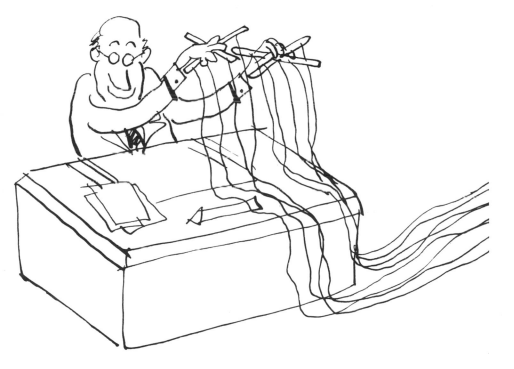

MANAGEMENT CONTROLLING PRINCIPLES AND STYLES

"Let us remember that the followers of the Lord Jesus Christ are called 'sheep' and the continuing need of any sheep is a shepherd. We recognize this spiritually and we appoint undershepherds but this is equally important in the practical outworkings of our lives."

Management Controlling Principles

One definition of management controlling is, "the work we engage in to check work in progress and complete it." This is one area of Christian work that perplexes me greatly. How have we come to assume that we can be thrown in together as a group of individuals with the view of accomplishing common goals without someone assuming the responsibility for checking and coordinating the work in progress? But often no one does. In our types of organization we come up with a whole series of people, it can be fifty or one hundred and twenty-five, allegedly banded together and moving toward an objective like the evangelization of a community and the planting of the church in that area. Yet, in the final outworking instead of moving in union and harmony, the tendency is for each man to follow the path of his own inclination. Dedicated men go in all kinds of directions with goals that may be similar but are seldom coordinated.

The point of management controlling is, once the goal has been identified, once the relationships have been determined, once the work has been assigned, once the decision-making power or authority has been clearly defined, to ensure that we all go in one direction and work in harmony. No one is more aware of the problems of control than I am and yet I still presume to emphasize that the problem can be overcome. Do not assume that your organization is so different, that everyone is just simply too individualistic. We *can* expect to achieve this kind of union towards our objective. It *can* be done.

Management control must be implemented in order that we can accomplish our common goal. How shall we describe missions and churches, generally? We have a man at the top, frequently insecure and very unsure of what he is supposed to do. Often he is so totally oblivious of the value of management controlling, that he simply assumes or hopes that everyone will move toward the objective when he exerts a little pressure and influence and commits the work to God in prayer. Frequently, when objectives are *not* being accomplished, but while there is work being done and signs of activity evident, those in positions of leadership do not take any action. But, as the situation deteriorates and worsens, men in leadership begin to be concerned. They begin to pray. They should go further and implement management control. An individual responsible for the group should begin to check the work in progress against the performance standards that have been established.

I think we harm our Christian workers in deference to their demands to be individualists, we let them wander all over the place without reining them in tight and controlling their activities and saying, "Here is the direction we are going. We are trying to accomplish this. Here is your role. Now play that role." We all have come into the Lord's work because of the strong goal-orientation. Individualism emerges after we are in the group, not before. It is not the result of what we were before we got into the group. We came into the group because we wanted to move in union with other men toward the accomplishment of the goal. What is the problem? The problem is leadership. There usually is not a man at the top who is so goal-oriented that he gives the order and says, "We are going to do this. Here is your role." He may eventually have to go back and say, "Excuse me, Joe, we blundered on the project. I am awfully sorry. Now let us try again and go towards this goal." But this seldom happens. Some of you may come from highly goal-oriented missions where there is adequate management pressure at the top to move people in unison, but generally speaking this is not so.

We must always respect people as human beings, not pieces of machinery, not just some inanimate object that you place in some place and say, "Do this," and he does it. No, these are human beings, but they are human beings who want to accomplish a goal.

Occasionally you will meet a Christian worker who does not want to accomplish anything. Sometimes you will have to remove him from the pursuit of this goal and send him home. If one of these men embezzled $60,000, you would remove him. If he becomes involved in heresy, you ship him off. But he can wander around ineffectively on the field, and we do not do anything about it. I want to insist that it is not his fault. It is the top man's fault; or maybe we should say, it is the *men* at the top.

So many things begin to merge here and come to the fore: the goal-orientation, organization, the job description, communications, establishing and maintaining human inter-relationships, the authority by which we manage. However, the persons who are wandering aimlessly around are not to blame. Let us remember that the followers of the Lord Jesus Christ are called "sheep" and the continuing need of any sheep is a shepherd. We recognize this spiritually and we appoint undershepherds but this is equally important in the practical outworkings of our lives.

Management controlling is concerned with ineffective and vague leadership. Admittedly, the longer the organization has been in existence, the more difficulties you are going to have. It can be changed! But without great effort. Still, it can be done provided we are willing to pay the price and the leaders are sufficiently goal-oriented and courageous.

The Establishment of Performance Standards

Do you know when management control begins with a missionary, or with a person taking over a Sunday School department in the church, or with the man who is taking the job in the office of the Bible Society, or with the one who is coming into a strategic position in the hospital? Performance standards must be started *before* he starts to work. Missionary societies need to do this with their candidates before they ever sign on the dotted line and the Home Board accepts them. Do you know what kind of men you will attract when you clearly state the objectives of the group and the responsibilities of each individual? You will attract the courageous, the goal-oriented, the self-effacing, the self-sacrificing. Always! But the standards have to be determined ahead of time. If they are not, and you have to go back and pick up the pieces, then it is more difficult. Even in an old organization where a man goes and comes when he desires, it can be done. One day a lady who has visited a number of mission fields, said to me, "Do you know the great tragedy on the mission field? The great tragedy is -- there is not *must!* No 'I *must* get up!' 'I *must* have my devotions.' 'I *must* study.' 'I *must* finish this language exam.' 'I *must* see these people.' 'I *must* prepare for this conference.'" Management controlling forces us to put the "must" back into our work.

Management controlling is concerned with having an agreement with the individual that these are the standards toward which we are aiming. These standards are not unilaterally determined and handed down to the individual. Mr. A., up at the top, does not come along to a worker and say, "Look, you are going to do such and such." How does he do it? Mr. A., either on the field or back in the homeland, comes along and says, "Now listen, our goal is this. Here are your gifts. Here is your calling according to your testimony. What standards of performance do you feel we should aim at together in order to accomplish this?" The man will always be more exacting with himself than you would be with him, if you were left to yourself to devise the standard unilaterally.

Then put it in writing. It is amazing how illiterate we become when it comes to management! We will not write things down! My first question to people with managerial problems is, "Does this fellow know his problem?" My second question is, "Is it written down and does he have a copy and do you have a copy?" The answer ninety-nine times out of a hundred is "No." *We must write down the standard of performance and give the person involved a copy.*

We who are in positions of leadership are required to love those under us supremely, but at the same time to hold them to the highest standards. The man at the top must constantly watch the performance of those under him. How many people should a man manage? A man should supervise only as many people as he can effectively manage. What happens when he cannot manage all of the people? Someone else should manage some of them. The people we usually elect to managerial positions are already so busy that they cannot possibly oversee and scrutinize the activities and procedures of others. But this is what is so absolutely essential.

Performance Measuring

The second demand is *performance measuring*. The man at the top must have some yardstick for measuring activities. What kind of measurements do we need? We need to know when a fellow gets up and when he goes to bed. We need to know how many days he takes to go on vacation. We need to know when he is going on furlough and when he is coming back. I have been in missions all of these years and I still do not understand how a missionary is permitted to just unilaterally determine, "I'm going home and I'm coming back. I'll let you know when." What kind of control is that?

Performance measuring is based on what we are doing and the goal we are collectively seeking to achieve. There are two elements: the standard of performance toward which we are aiming, and the man whose performance is being measured.

Psychology tells us that one of the basic drives of the human being is his desire to achieve. There is a fire burning in the breast of every man to achieve something before he dies. This is especially true of every man in your mission or he would not be a missionary. He would be back home earning money and storing it away and living comfortably. If he seems to fight against management, he is not fighting because he is afraid that the superintendent or director is going to help him achieve something. He is fighting because he is afraid this person is going *to keep him from* achieving something. He is so individualistic that he does not want the missionary society to hinder him from accomplishing something for the Lord and His Kingdom. Management is not there to obstruct. While we push decisions down the ladder, what else do we send down? Concern, help, direction. The man at the top should be able to say, ''Look, the whole purpose of our being banded together, having superiors and subordinates and job descriptions and organizational charts and decisions made, is to facilitate the accomplishment of the thing that God has given you to do.

Performance Evaluating

Third, *performance evaluating* is a little different from performance measuring. In my thinking, in performance measuring we are concerned about *one* man. In performance evaluating we are concerned about appraising the relative value of this man's activities in relation to the activities of other men. This becomes even more difficult than performance measuring because with performance measuring we are concerned with one individual; but with performance evaluating we are concerned with many individuals and their activities.

Performance Correcting

In *performance correcting* we are concerned with coaching, with providing the ''how'' to people and, where necessary, correcting a situation that may have gone awry, always with the objective in view. A manager must not correct simply to satisfy his own desires or wishes. That is why goal-orientation is a necessity.

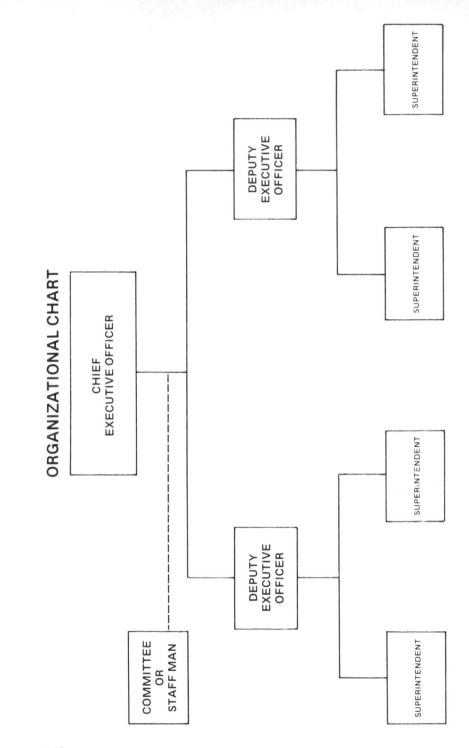

ORGANIZATIONAL CHART

CHIEF EXECUTIVE OFFICER

DEPUTY EXECUTIVE OFFICER

DEPUTY EXECUTIVE OFFICER

COMMITTEE OR STAFF MAN

SUPERINTENDENT

SUPERINTENDENT

SUPERINTENDENT

SUPERINTENDENT

MANAGEMENT STYLES

Scientific Management

There are several styles of management. The *scientific management style* has maximum concern for accomplishment but people are merely tools for the accomplishment. This management style is a laborious or toilsome type of management. This is where people are nothing more than necessary instruments or machines to accomplish tasks. This sort of management style often develops in religious situations. Generally it is the product of the strong natural leader, though not always. It may be the product of a highly insecure but domineering leader. Scientific management has maximum concern for accomplishment but a regard for people that is sub-human.

Country Club Management

The other extreme is *country club management* which says that the thing we are concerned about most is the happiness of these people. Whether we do anything or not is quite irrelevant. This is where everyone works together around a swimming pool with tall cold drinks right at their elbow. Everybody is just happy, and at any gathering, or any situation, the whole concern is for happiness. This was epitomized in President Lyndon Johnson's speech one time when he turned to a heckler and said, "Why don't you people be happy?" -- as though happiness were all that counts.

Impoverished Management

Another style, unfortunately, is *impoverished management.* This is where a man is neither motivated by a very great respect for the dignity of human personalities under his care, nor is he very much concerned about getting the product out the back door and on the train and shipped. Do not make the mistake of assuming that this kind of management style does not exist in Christian circles. It does. Often enough many pastors fit this category. They are satisfied to maintain things as they are, concerned only that their job is secure.

Compromise Management

Another style of management is a *compromise management*. It is neither dynamic nor is it dormant. It is active, it is alive, but barely. It is a middle-of-the-road kind of management. The idea is that we want you to be happy, but not too happy. We will do anything to make you happy if it does not mean too much trouble. Certainly we want to achieve something. We really want to evangelize this country, but we are not going to sweat or toil about it. We are not going to get excited about it or "hot under the collar." In a survey that has been done by UCLA, it was discovered from the estimate of thousands of managers in top-middle-lower echelons in America that 65% of industrial managers adjust their management style to this position. What does that mean in regard to Christian managers? What percentage of people involved in religious work use compromise management?

Pendulum-swing Management

There are other alternatives, but one thing that often happens is the wide-arc pendulum-swing where a fellow swings back and forth from one style of management to the other. An inspirational sermon shakes his complacency, he makes sudden changes and clamps down on everybody. The result is that everybody becomes tense. Then someone comes along and says to him, "If you don't be good, we will not re-elect you." So, swinging back over to a country-club position, he apologizes and seeks to smooth out the situation. That is the wide-arc pendulum-swing. Its chief characteristics are vacillation and inconsistency.

Concern Management

There is another position which is best. This is a combination of concern for people in its maximum manifestation with a concern for production or accomplishment to its absolute maximum. This is the management style epitomized in the Lord Jesus Christ. He demonstrated the perfect combination of concern for people with concern for accomplishment.

There are three basic issues in any management style: creativity, commitment and conflict. These ingredients must be present in any wholesomely managed situation. What do these various management styles do to the various issues?

Creativity. What does Scientific Management do to it? Remember this is a laborious, toilsome type of management. Every effort is made to accomplish and produce without showing any concern for the workers. In one sense this is a very stimulating environment for creativity. However, it stimulates creativity in an anti-organizational way. It provokes people to figure out ways to beat the system.

Commitment. Scientific Management also creates high commitment, but also in anti-organizational ways. Usually people within the group form themselves around an insurrectionist who says, "Who cares for this society? Look how they are treating us! Let us join together and fight them."

Conflict. Conflict is a necessary ingredient in human relationships. It was Lord Cromwell who said to one of his aides, "For heaven's sake, man, say 'no,' so I'll know there are two of us!" There must be wholesome conflict. But scientific management merely suppresses conflict. If a worker has a complaint, he is rebuked and told to keep quiet.

What does Country-Club Management do with these elements? Country-Club Management has a concern for happiness. As to creativity, it stifles it. You have no creativity in country-club management because everyone wants things "as is" and they are not willing to do any forward thinking. As to commitment, it creates very high commitment, but in narrow pro-organizational ways. This creates the centric group because it is oblivious to the goal. Country-Club Management is never occupied with a worthwhile goal. Its goal is every man's happiness. As to conflict, this management smothers it. Everything is fine. Please do not disturb.

And what about Impoverished Management? Creativity does not exist. You do not have any creativity, any imagination, any forward thinking. As to commitment, the only commitment that you have is the commitment of survival. You are only committed insofar as it is necessary to keep your donors from dropping you and to keep your mission from sending you home. As to conflict, it produces absolute neutrality. There is no differing of opinions. There is no peppering interaction that produces creativity and dynamics.

The Compromise Management position characterizes most religious organizations. What does it do to creativity? Creativity is entirely directed towards personal survival. It does exist, not with respect to the work but with respect to personal survival. It is my work; these are my donors; this is my calling. Commitment, however, tends to be high, simply because in the compromise position a man has to be committed in order to survive. He is neither secure in what he is accomplishing, nor in his relationship with other people. So instead, he finds his security in a highly personalized description of his task: "God led me to this place." So, what does this do to the conflict? Whenever there is conflict there is splintering and there is compromise. There is neither substantial goal-orientation to insure that the conflict is creative and wholesome, nor is there sufficient adjustment for keeping everyone happy. So this fellow gives a little, and somebody else gives a little, and the manager gives here and gives there.

What about Concern Management? Creativity is high and stimulating. Not only because a person knows that his boss recognizes value in his dignity, but because he knows that the whole organization with which he is associated is out to accomplish the goal that he has personally espoused. Commitment is very high because, as an individual, he has a stake and a voice and he is personally involved. Effective management does not reduce involvement but increases involvement in decision making. Regarding *conflict*, warm interaction and a sharp exchange of ideas often occur because issues are confronted head-on. They are not suppressed. There must be a warm conflict, not personal hatred nor personal animosity, but personal inter-action that is stimulating and dynamic. Otherwise, one person with a group of puppets or figures could do as much as a whole group is doing. Conflict is where persons are pushed to be individuals on their own. Someone has well said, "Conformity in behavior in an organization is essential, conformity in ideas in an organization is tragic." Conflict does not necessarily mean fighting; perhaps "creative tension" would better describe it. Interaction, the idea of each person acting on the other, brings us up to our best. Generally we suppress interaction because the man at the top is afraid it is going to reflect on some of his deficiencies.

Conformity of behavior is essential, but conformity in ideas is tragic. When we conform in our ideas, and everybody has to think the same things, we stagnate. Many missionary societies are in a state of stagnation today. From time to time the sharing of our ideas on various aspects of our work, such as finance and furloughs, produces a healthy situation. We need to encourage and stimulate our co-workers to express themselves. However, we do not implement everything that occurs to us. We must have a system of evaluation, scrutinizing, appraising, and testing before we implement. I talked to a candidate sometime ago who had been turned down by a mission. I may be wrong, but my estimate of the situation was that they turned him down because he was too creative. I do not think he will go to the mission field now. That is too bad.

Let us picture in our mind a missionary organization of three hundred people represented by twenty-five charts. When new workers come in, usually they are placed in the lower echelon of the chart. They have a specific function and assignment, and, incidentally, it should be made clear to the new workers that even though they are low on the chart they are not inferior socially. Each position is vital to the function and goal of the organization; but unfortunately, most people think only of status.

A new worker is accepted by the missionary organization. In a lot of missions they say, "So you are joining our group. For a year, or two years, you will not have any vote; for a term you will be a junior missionary and will not have any say. Please keep silent." Is this right? Or is there a better way? Do we need a screening process where the mentality and the goal and the function of the group is adequately represented to this fellow so that when he comes in he is a part of the organization? Why do we stifle? It is because we are afraid, we are insecure, we are not sure where we stand and where we are going, what we are doing and how to do it. The moment new people come into our mission, or into our church, we are changing our mission and our church. The addition of one personality to our church alters that church. We have to screen so that we do not get people in who are undesirable, but let us determine what is undesirable.

WHAT NOW?

"Management offers tools that can help you if you implement them and use them. But the very best tools are useless unless we use them."

The purpose of this book was to INTRODUCE the subject of management to Christian workers. Do not assume that you know everything about management because you have read this book! If this is all you have ever studied or read on the subject of management, then you know very little. To give anyone the impression (or to be under the impression yourself) that you are a knowledgeable person in the field of management will only lead to trouble. This book is an introduction to the subject. What you do after this is of real significance. Hundreds and hundreds of people have come to management seminars that I have taught. However, we find that only 10% to 15% of those who attend ever do anything about what they learn. Many people go away and talk about it; they have been impressed, and some are even excited about the relevance of much of this material. But that is not enough! A little knowledge is very dangerous, particularly when it comes to management. This sort of thing takes work. Work. You have to experiment. You have to revise it. You have to adapt it. You have to discuss it. It is worthwhile if you persevere.

Another point is to not assume that this is a substitute for something else. It is not a substitute for prayer, nor for the fullness of the Holy Spirit. Management offers tools that can help you if you implement them and use them. But the very best tools are useless unless we use them.

Do not start telling people how much you know. You will alienate them. They will resent your possessing knowledge that they do not have, and you might even get your neck in a good tight noose if you are not very careful. Do something before you do a lot of talking. Start with yourself -- with your job description, your own objectives, your own organizational chart. Start with an effort to appraise your own communication. Start with yourself. You will do this best by example, not by word, and if you apply words too soon, you are going to be in real trouble.

Many management teachers have emphasized that if you are ever to do anything with management, you will begin it within two weeks after the basic exposure. What you do not begin within two weeks, you will probably not do anything about. Three months from now you will go right back to the "tyranny of the urgent" at the expense of the important. It happens to hundreds and hundreds of people, not just in Christian work, but in industry too, all the time. Young executives go away to a seminar. They come back and their desks are piled high. Immediately they feel that they must deal with everything that is on their desks. These are the urgent matters lying at hand. Management is important, but the pressures of the moment push all they received at the seminar away into the background.

Write a report on the helpful information you have received relative to your own work and your own situation. Start with yourself and your own work. A written report will put in solid memorable form what you have received, and it is a good way to relate the information, or relay the information from the shelf to other people.

Having worked out an organizational chart, do not expect to push the ideas you have learned and believe to be useful up your chart. It will not work. Begin where you are. Then educate in other directions first, that is, down and sideways. There may even be the desire to change the constitution of your organization. Don't! Start applying the management principles in the organization as it is.

To summarize, here is WHAT NOT TO DO:

1. Do not assume that you know everything about management.
2. Do not assume that management is a substitute for prayer or the fullness of the Holy Spirit.
3. Do not go to the organization and tell them how much they need to adopt these principles.
4. Do not expect to push these ideas up your organizational chart.
5. Do not try to change the constitution of your organization.

Here is WHAT TO DO:

1. Start within two weeks after reading this book, and start with yourself.
2. Write a report to your boss.
3. Begin to educate in four directions, i.e. down, sideways, and finally up.
4. Set aside some time to study management further.
5. Start a file of management information.

BIBLIOGRAPHY

ALEXANDER, JOHN W. *Managing Our Work.* (Downers Grove, Illinois: Inter-Varsity Press, 1972. 84 pages, illustrated, bibliography.)
Deals with work management in the areas of planning, execution, review, continuing and growth management.

APPLEY, LAWRENCE A. *Formula For Success - A Core Concept of Management.* (New York: American Management Association. 1974, 138 pages.)
Deals with the problems that confront executives. The basic concept is that a manager must get things done through others by leading a group toward the attainment of common goals.

BATTEN, JOE D. *Tough-Minded Management.* (New York: American Management Ass'n. 1969. 218 pages, index.)
Shows how the manager tackles his duties of planning, delegating and controlling. The methods used to get things done through people, how to introduce change when necessary, the kind of men with whom he surrounds himself.

BRUCE, A.B. *The Training of the Twelve.* (Grand Rapids: Kregel Publishers. 1971. 552 pages, index. Reprint.)
Written about the turn of the century by the great Glasgow theologian treating thoroughly the Lord Jesus Christ and His work with His apostles.

BUTT, HOWARD. *The Velvet Covered Brick - Christian Leadership in an Age of Rebellion.* (New York: Harper & Row. 1973. 186 pages, notes.)
This book takes unfashionable words, authority and submission, and dares to suggest their relevance today. It is deeply Christian and personal in tone; yet even ''like-minded souls'' will find it refreshing and full of surprises.

CLASSEN, WILLARD. *Learning To Lead.* (Scotdale, PA: Herald Press. 1963. 112 pages.)
Discusses the characteristics of immature and mature groups, communication, decision making, goal setting, and evaluation.

CLASSEN, WILLARD. *Learn To Lead - Leader's Guide.* (to be used with above textbook.)

COLEMAN, ROBERT E. *The Master Plan of Evangelism.* (New York: Fleming H. Revell.)

A popular study of the relationship of Jesus and the Twelve. Written by the professor of Evangelism at Asbury Seminary. A must book!

DAYTON, EDWARD R. *God's Purpose/Man's Plans.* (Monrovia, CA: MARC. 1971. A workbook.)

A logic diagramming technique called PERT is described as a useful planning tool. It discusses planning and goal setting as a response to God's purpose for the church and individual Christians.

DRUCKER, PETER F. *The Effective Executive.* (London: Heinemann, also New York: Harper & Row. 1966. 148 pages, index.)

Drucker identifies five "talents," knitting them together by effective decision making. How to develop these talents forms the main body of the book.

GANGEL, KENNETH O. *Competent to Lead.* (Chicago: Moody Press. 1974. 144 pages, illustrated, bibliography.)

Dr. Gangel has touched the very nerve center of the work of the local church. He has grappled realistically, practically, and exceedingly helpfully with the issues that confront every leader in Christian work. A must!

GROSSMAN, LEE. *The Change Agent.* (New York: American Management Ass'n. 1974. 168 pages.)

Gives pointers on how to make meaningful changes happen that are right for you and your organization.

HODGES, MELVIN L. *Grow Toward Leadership.* (Chicago: Moody Press. 1969. revised edition. 63 pages.)

This book focuses mainly on the area of spiritual leadership. The author cites examples and principles of executive responsibility as found in the Word of God.

KEPNER, CHARLES H. and TREGOE, BENJAMIN B. *The Rational Manager - A Systematic Approach to Problem Solving and Decision Making.* (New York: McGraw-Hill. 1965. 275 pages, illustrated, bibliography, index.)

The authors have developed clear concepts and procedures that enable a manager to approach every problem systematically and to solve it efficiently. This is a practical, not a theoretical, book.

KOLIVOSKY, MICHAEL E. and TAYLOR, LAURENCE J. *Why Do You See It That Way?* (Hillsdale, Michigan: Hillsdale College. 1972. 2nd printing. 147 pages, illustrated.)

Contains principles of perception: most applicable principles for guidelines in inter-personal relationships. An excellent book!

KOONTZ, HAROLD and O'DONNELL, CYRIL. *Principles of Management - An Analysis of Managerial Functions.* (New York: McGraw-Hill. 1972. 5th edition, 748 pages, illustrated, case incidents, references.)
Furnishes a framework of basic knowledge organized and presented under the functions of planning, organizing, staffing, directing, and controlling.

LAIRD, DONALD A. and LAIRD, ELEANOR C. *The Techniques of Delegating.* (New York: McGraw-Hill. 1957.)
The classic and best ever written on delegation. Don't let the date fool you. It is as current as can be as to strategy and principles.

MACKENZIE, R. ALEC. *The Time Trap.* (New York: American Management Ass'n. 1972. 195 pages, illustrated, notes, index.)
The author has packed this book with practical easy-to-apply tips that you can use to make yourself many times more productive than you ever thought possible.

MAGER, ROBERT F. *Goal Analysis.* (Belmont, California: Fearon Publishers. 1972. 136 pages, illustrated, selected references.)
Helps in answering questions like: What do you do about the affective domain? Why don't they have the right attitude? How can I motivate them? How can I deepen their appreciation?

NICHOLS, SUE. *Words on Target.* (New York: McGraw-Hill. 1957. 235 pages, bibliography, index.)
A valuable primer for anyone who wants to write and speak effectively. One of the best on this subject!

ODEIRNE, GEORGE S. *Management by Objectives.* (New York: Pitman. 1965.)
An old one, but a good one. Management by objectives starts here.

ROGERS, EVERETT M. and SHOEMAKER, F. FLOYD. *Communication of Innovations - A Cross-Cultural Approach.* (New York: The Free Press. 1971. Second edition, 476 pages, illustrated, bibliography, index.)
Integrates diffusion research with the scientific study of

human communication; stresses communication concepts and frameworks in our analysis of the diffusion process.

SCHALLER, LYLE E. *The Change Agent.* (New York: Abingdon Press. 1972. 207 pages, notes, index.)
Deals concisely with identifying change, planning for change, anticipating and managing conflict caused by change, etc. An excellent book!

STONE, W. CLEMENT. *The Success System That Never Fails.* (Englewood Cliffs, New Jersey: Prentice Hall. 1962. 252 pages, illustrated, bibliography, index.)
Shows you how to do twice as much in half the time, how temporary failures can become permanent success, how to have the courage to enter the unknown... and much, much more.